THIS GIRL WALKS INTO A BAR

A Women's Guide to Professional Bartending and Home Mixology

Written by Jordan Catapano
Designed by Jocelyn Dunn Muhlbach

Library of Congress Cataloging-in-Publication Data:
This Girl Walks Into A Bar
ISBN 978-0615594811
2011910918
Second edition

Designed by Petit Bureau Design Studio.

Dedicated with love to
Frankie, Luigi, Natalie,
Cortney, Mom, and Dad

TABLE OF CONTENTS

INTRODUCTION

CHAPTERS

100 COCKTAIL RECIPE FLASH CARDS

INTRODUCTION: THIS GIRL'S STORY

Night after night at the bar some woman was bound to ask how I got into bartending and how she might too. And when making drinks for guests in our home, my friends would remark how fortunate I was to have professional bartending experience. I began to realize that there is way too much mystery surrounding making cocktails, whether formally at a bar or informally in the comfort of one's home. It was time to write a book that demystified the process and made the art of mixology accessible to anyone. I began my research and discovered that only three types of bar books existed: those thicker than the yellow pages, listing every cocktail since the Paleolithic Age, coffee table bar books with glossy portraits of murky unidentifiable drinks, or frilly pink "girl's night out" books that help ladies match their cocktail's color to their toenail polish. Ugh. My book needed to be practical, relevant, and easy to use.

With the help of my amazing business partner and graphic designer sister, Jocelyn, we've created a fun yet functional all-in-one bartending guide designed for anyone who wants the lucrative career of tending bar, or simply aspires to mix cocktails like a master at home. College students, homemakers, business people, or anyone looking to supplement an income, change jobs, or spice up a social life will benefit from this book.

The first section is designed for those who want a professional bartending gig. Our reader gets true and sometimes shocking personal stories, insider tips on how to deal with everything from drunks who hump barstools to customers who don't tip, warnings about all things alcohol related, and even a shiny set of non-pink flash cards.

The second section of our book is for the woman who wants to nurture her inner mixologist. You'll learn how to create original drinks, how to throw a variety of cocktail parties at home, and how to make and shake drinks like a pro. After reading this book (don't skip the first section!), no one will ever guess you've never actually set foot behind a real bar!

Now, pour yourself a glass of wine, find a comfortable chair to read in, and begin your new venture into the world of cocktails.

Cheers!

PROFESSIONAL BARTENDING

Not long ago, the dark, dingy world of bartending was dominated by men. Society considered them the best and only candidates for such a job. Working where smoke burned your eyes, liquor stained your hands, and the nightly audience consisted of foul-mouthed heavy drinkers, was no place for a lady.

Things have changed. The smoke has cleared and the atmosphere has evolved to adapt to a lively female clientele. Today you can walk into any watering hole, five star or dive bar, and find a woman slinging drinks with the best of them. Woman have broken up their share of bar fights and dodged many a hurled highball. In my humble opinion, there's no one better for the job than a broad. Why you ask...?

When God created woman, she gave us three unique gifts: the gift of childbirth, the gift of multiple orgasms, and the gift of multi-tasking.

Yes, we're just as grateful as you are. What would life be like without our ability to multi-task?! And it's this particular treasure that makes us the perfect candidates for bartending.

Night after night, a bartender juggles hundreds of drink orders, dozens of food requests, and ten different conversations at a time (varying in depth and intelligence). The key to success is balancing the Four S's: **Smarts, Speed, Sass, and Sex.**

These "S's" will help you to manage that old cliché that couldn't be truer. A bartender wears the hat of a priest, a shrink, and a bosom buddy. You'll get to know your customers better than many of their own spouses do. The only difference is that while you're listening to Wendy go on and on about her breakup and to Walter complain endlessly about his day, you're expected to whip up three Apple Martinis, an Old Fashioned and two Blended Cadillacs without batting your eyelashes... well, batting those can be a good thing. But you're not supposed to miss a beat.

THE FOUR S'S

If you think you're lacking one, or even all four of the S's, stop right here because as a woman, you were born with them. And when you combine these ingredients, you become a lethal weapon behind the bar.

SMARTS.

First of all, you have them (gobs!) because you're reading this book. Second, it doesn't take a PhD to master mixology. Can you speak in complete sentences? Do you have good instincts? Are you good with people? Can you add and subtract? Then you have more than enough brainpower to excel at this job.

SASS.

There's not a woman around who doesn't possess some sass in her DNA, or use it on a regular basis. Remember when you finessed your way out of that speeding ticket? Or talked your way into that night club? You're using the same skills to be a stellar bartender. You gotta be a little bit bitch, a little bit angel, and a whole lotta smart-ass rolled into one. With time, you'll become an expert in knowing when to pull back and when to pour it on.

SPEED.

A busy bar demands that you keep moving all night, so maintaining a sense of urgency is essential (you know, it's like sipping your latte, applying your mascara and sending a text before the traffic light turns green). Most bar spaces are cramped, especially when shared with other bartenders, and it's here where our swinging curves and flexibility pay off. You'll also notice that people won't be able to take their eyes off you as you whiz around the bar producing one perfect cocktail after another. Your speed and grace will be intoxicating (payoff for all those soccer practices and ballet recitals as a kid).

SEX.

Forget the implants and hair extensions. The real recipe for sex appeal is all in the eye contact. Looking into customers' eyes when you set their drink down and sincerely acknowledging their presence is all it takes to make them feel special. With the warmth of your smile and the twinkle in your eye, they'll be as smitten as a kitten for the rest of the night.

TAKE THE QUIZ ON THE NEXT PAGE TO SEE IF YOU'RE READY TO QUIT YOUR JOB AND EXPLORE BARTENDING!

SHOULD I QUIT MY DAY JOB?

(Check all that apply)

- ○ Your vacation time is so pathetic that the closest you'll get to a tropical island is drinking a Mai Tai in your bathtub.

- ○ You're so bored at the office that you've memorized the rotation of the temp's outfits and feel secretly outraged if she forgets the order.

- ○ You hum along to Muzak and have even considered downloading a few favorites.

- ○ When stationed at the fitting room, sorting "go-backs" with a folding board, you obsess over how, at this point in your life, you ended up in a fitting room, sorting "go-backs" with a folding board.

- ○ Your boss is as smart as a paper clip and should have handed the job over to you years ago.

- ○ At parties you lie about what you do for a living.

- ○ The CEO has no plans to remove the glass ceiling.

- ○ Of course your retail job values your customer service, your sales, and your loyalty. But how many credit cards have customers opened this week?

- ○ You've convinced yourself that fluorescent lighting is a sufficient source of vitamin D.

- ○ You look forward to trips to the bathroom simply for a change of scenery.

- ○ On Saturdays at about 3:00pm you start thinking about your job again and decide the weekend might as well be over.

- ○ You stay late, you work your ass off, and once again at the end of the year, you'll be handsomely rewarded with a booze cruise and company mug.

- ○ Water cooler conversations have run so dry that filling the tank with vodka is the only imaginable solution.

- ○ Your dry cleaning bills are a quarter of your salary.

- ○ Ordering that second Chardonnay at Rob's birthday lunch has you pegged as the office drunk.

- ○ Your weekends are spent doing everything that you can't do during the week because you're at work all &%$#-ing day long.

If you checked one or more of these reasons, this book is going to save you from driving a mechanical pencil into your eye, or arriving drunk at your retirement party and telling everyone off. If you didn't check any, well, congratulations. Your life is perfect and we hate you.

Regardless of why you're looking for a change of occupation, now's the time to do it. We have a job in mind that you'll actually look forward to going to. Imagine a shortened work-week, no 9 to 5 (or 8 to 7!), and the cash flow to pay a mortgage and get the latest Prada shoes. Begin with Chapter One and find out how your life can become a whole lot sweeter!

1

CHAPTER ONE
THE TOP TEN REASONS TO BECOME A BARTENDER

1. Cash
And lots of it. These days the typical tip per drink is a dollar…and believe us, it adds up faster than the calories in a Starbucks Frappuccino. You won't have to wait two weeks anymore to buy that La Perla Lingerie. You can get it the very next day without even touching your Visa.

2. Respect
You have a skill that the average person lacks, and it will bring you admiration and high regard. On a busy Friday night the only thing standing between a man and his thirst is you. This gives you power. People will treat you more like a celebrity "It Girl" than simply a server.

3. Freedom
Because your shift starts in the late afternoon/early evening, your day will be open to develop other interests. We've met many bartenders who attend law school, teach, or pursue acting during the day. Your flexible hours and piles of money will leave the door to your future wide open.

PERSONAL STORY: *Lauren*

Right after college I decided to move from Los Angeles to Ohio for graduate school, far from the free meals, rent, and Netflix at mom and dad's house. It only took two days in my new city to find work again as a bartender!

4. Job Security
People drink when the economy is thriving, and probably more when it's taking a nose-dive. In other words, there will always be a need for bartenders. It's a talent you can take to any city in any part of the world and find work (okay, maybe not Siberia). And it's probably one of the few jobs where you don't need to ass kiss, paper push or coffee fetch your way to a starting salary of over $70,000.

5. No 9 to 5
If you're like us, sitting behind a desk five days a week sounds about as fun as swimming in Lake Michigan in January. Bartending allows you to create your own schedule and work as much or as little as you want. At a busy joint, you can work three nights, date four, and still save for a cute condo in the city.

6. You're the Boss

It's you who decides which new vodkas to carry, how late the kitchen stays open, which servers to send home first, and what obnoxiously inebriated customers to permanently ban. Since the bar's owner or manager can't be there every minute, he depends on you to make decisions on his behalf. He may not be able to make a drink to save his life but he knows that the livelihood of his business depends on the liquor, not the chicken. This gives you a lot of authority without the added pressure of running the place.

7. Connections

You never know who is going to step into your bar one night, take a sip of your divine cocktail, and decide to become a regular. She may be the mayor or a big movie producer. He may be the chief of police or a coach for your NBA team. Be nice to customers because you never know when you may need their help.

8. Chit Chat

Okay, technically you're working. But where else do you get paid to stand around and talk to people about their lives? During the busy nights, there's not much time for gossip, but on the slower ones you can dish the dirt and discuss the latest political scandal. This ain't happening in no cubicle.

9. Make People Happy

People come to bars for all sorts of reasons. Sometimes it's to hang out with loved ones; sometimes it's to escape them. With experience you'll learn to gage when your customers want to talk, when they want to listen, and when they just want to be left the hell alone. Chances are that with your professionalism and friendliness, they'll leave in a better mood then when they came in. Of course, a couple of your killer martinis running through their veins and they're bound to cheer up too!

10. Free Drinks

Every place has a different policy. Never sneak a drink 'cause that can get you into trouble. Try to find a bar where it's okay for someone to buy you one. Customers like to do this and it's nice to be able to accept it (and of course, drink it!).

PERSONAL STORY: *Kavita*

A fellow bartender was having legal trouble, and she told her story to a regular who was a lawyer. He took her case to court pro bono and won! I have a box full of business cards and will hang onto them long after I've hung up my martini shaker.

2

CHAPTER TWO
BREAKING INTO THE BUSINESS

Once you're in, you're in, but getting through that door can take some creativity. Here are the five most common paths to making your debut behind the bar.

Bartending School

These schools are very popular, but be careful. Schools can be a waste of time and money. Sometimes this can actually work against you when applying for a job. It's like Candy Striping for a summer in high school and then expecting to scrub in for open-heart surgery. Sure, you spend a week learning every drink created since the Paleolithic Age. But that means little to the owner of a restaurant who wants you to be street smart, not book smart. Now, if you feel you have to take some classes, remember that those tuitions are often negotiable.

Waiting Tables

As a server, you already have the basic skills needed to successfully tend bar: multi-tasking, customer service, communicating with the front and back of the house, and dealing with that asshole at table 8 who can't stop staring at your chest (as lovely as it is).

So why not make the leap to a more lucrative position? If you are currently waitressing, ask the manager if you can train behind the bar. You'll be an extra pair of hands for the bartenders while learning the nuts and bolts of the craft.

Lying Through Your Teeth

Ever lied about your weight? Piece of cake. Bedpost notches don't match your sex resumé? No one has to know. If you're an expert fibber and have hosted your share of cocktail parties, you can probably get away with winging it behind the bar for a little bit. But if you've never made two drinks in one shaker and filled both glasses to the rim, you'll be exposed faster than a fake Louis Vuitton. Your embellished resumé may look believable, but your inexperience will be revealed as soon as you grab the ice scoop. Proceed with caution when straying from the truth with this one.

PERSONAL STORY: *Lindsay*

When I was waitressing, I noticed the bartenders pulling in tons of cash. To persuade my manager to let me start training behind the bar, I offered to come in off the clock. After four weeks I knew enough to quit my waitressing position and immediately landed my first gig as a bartender.

> "If you're an expert fibber and have hosted your share of cocktail parties, you can probably get away with winging it behind the bar."

The 3-Day Cram

Remember pulling those all-nighters for big exams, when you'd drink a tank of coffee and consume a small candy store in order to stay awake? In the back of this book we've listed the 100 drinks you need to know to bartend. For those of you who can't stand the thought of returning to work on Monday, there's an even smaller list we've prepared in Chapter 12 for The 3-Day Cram. It's called the TOP 15. Look for the TOP 15 icon on the relevant drinks. These are the drinks you'll make over and over and over again each and every night. Memorize these and you'll be ready for your bartending debut in a matter of days. See Chapter 12 for your weekend itinerary.

Cocktail Party 101

If you aren't in a huge hurry to acquire a bartending job, you can teach yourself how to bartend by hosting three different parties over time: Intro to Mixers, Intermediate Soiree, and Advanced Shindig. These gatherings will not only give you enough skills to land a professional bartending job, but will very likely make you everyone's favorite hostess. See Chapter 13.

PERSONAL STORY: *Natalie*

There once was a new bartender whom I suspected had never set foot behind a bar (she cut limes like a dizzy lumberjack) As acting manager, I asked her to show me her version of a Lemon Drop. Hands shaking, forehead sweaty, she mixed together a bit of vodka and a squeeze of lemon. Logical? Yes. Correct? Hardly. She then strained the drink into a martini glass, barely filling it half way. Even an experienced bartender might be a little short on a drink when making three at once, but never one. She was gone by the end of the day.

A Bartender's **TIP**

Before you sign up for an online bartending school, be sure video tutorials will be available. A picture is worth 1,000 words. A video is worth a job.

3

CHAPTER THREE
FINDING THE RIGHT JOINT

If your rent is past due and all you've got for dinner is that box of stale crackers in the cupboard, take the first bartending offer that comes your way. But if time allows, search for a gig with the right fit for your lifestyle. Check out these pros and cons and see what resonates with you.

Independently Owned (Mom & Pops, Dive Bars)

PROS

Regulars.
A repeat clientele makes you feel like you're going to work to hang out with friends, and they generally keep your tip average high.

Adjustable Hours.
Because the bar is your boss' bread and butter, she doesn't want you standing around if there's no money coming in. Some nights you'll be able to bail hours early.

Free Pouring.
This means that you don't have to insult your customer by measuring out his whiskey in an itsy bitsy teeny tiny one ounce container called a "jigger." You just eyeball it.

Attire.
Chances are you won't be stuck in some sort of vest that's patterned and built like industrial strength carpet. Jeans paired with the bar's T-shirt is common.

Relationships.
The turnover is low and the big boss understands your worth. You're not just a number to corporate headquarters 2,000 miles away.

CONS

Benefits.
Not many mom and pops can offer you premium or premier or PPO health insurance, a 401(K), or profit-sharing.

Ownership.
Often the owners of these places are very hands-on. If you like them, great. If not, there'll be problems.

Stability.
If this bar is the one and only of its kind, there won't be sister stores to help make payroll during tough times.

Regulars.
Yes, we mention it as a pro, but the flip side is that you may not like those four grannies who sidle up to the bar every day at five to share a Chardonnay and a bowl of pretzels.

PERSONAL STORY: *Alyssa*

At the mom & pop joint where I used to work, especially busy nights would stress out my boss. To counter his nerves, he'd come behind the bar, fix himself a drink, and hover like a fruit fly. Then he'd start pointing out customers who needed a drink, as if I didn't know!

> "Having experience with a company that people know about is extremely beneficial. It's a stamp of approval that helps you get in the next door."

Chain Restaurants

PROS

Benefits.
If you're considered a full time employee you often can qualify for health care. Look into investment and retirement plans too if you plan on working for the company long term.

Well-Oiled Machine.
There's not much guessing to how things operate at these large companies. You'll learn the protocol for everything from folding napkins to garnishing a cup of soup. And if you come across something that stumps you, your manager or your manager's manager can always look at the employee handbook.

Stability.
It takes a lot more than a slow weekend for these bars to file for bankruptcy. If the numbers are low for a few months, you might feel it in your pocketbook, but it's not likely that you'll show up for work and find the doors chained shut.

Name Recognition.
Years and years from now when you decide you've made your truckloads of money, you may try a new career. Having experience with a company that people know about is extremely beneficial. It's a stamp of approval that helps you get in the next door.

The Chain.
If you move neighborhoods, towns, or even states, Human Resources will help you make a smooth transition to a new location. Some will even pay for the moving costs.

CONS

Jiggers.
There aren't too many corporate spots that will let you free pour (eyeballing the needed amount of liquor for a drink). Imagine the chef coming out of the kitchen with your hamburger meat and stuffing it into a measuring cup to be certain you weren't getting a milifraction of an ounce more than you were paying for. Yeah. Not a good feeling.

Uniforms.
A lot of spots require wearing a name-tag, goofy button, tie, lederhosen, a shirt that says "Boobies" (well not that word exactly but you know who we mean), or some other type of "flair."

Corporate Stuff.
Secret shoppers, discount cards, 2 for 1's, drink promotions, and servers with scripted greetings.

PERSONAL STORY: *Cara*

I worked at a place where you'd get in trouble if you didn't give each customer a detailed description of the breadbasket's contents. Seriously. It's just bread… not Chanel's spring collection.

Night Clubs

PROS

Busy.
Once these places get going, they don't stop. The money will pile up quickly and the night will zoom by.

Fun.
There's music, go-go dancers, incredible people-watching…not to mention the chance to bartend in a bustier, false eyelashes, and platform shoes.

Easy Customer Service.
No one expects anything from you except a drink. Hell, you don't even have to smile and you'll still get a tip.

Large Employee Base.
If you get asked out for a hot date a few hours before your shift begins, finding someone to cover for you is usually quite easy.

CONS

Late Nights.
Your shifts start well into the evening, which is great if you're a night owl, or pursuing another career during the day. But getting off of work at 4am is just terrible for fighting fine lines and wrinkles.

Tip pools.
Splitting the money evenly at the end of the night is only fair if everyone has worked as hard as you have.

No Down Time.
There's barely a bathroom break.

Seedy.
We've witnessed our share of cocaine parties in the bathroom and sexual escapades in corner booths. Stepping over used condoms and piles of vomit gets old quickly.

Conventions Centers / Sports Arenas / Ball Parks

PROS

High Hourly.
Usually these places offer an hourly wage that is considerably higher than your minimum wage restaurant job.

Flexibility.
You have the opportunity to work when you want to work without committing to a regular schedule. For some events management will need 10 bartenders and for others they'll need 100. Answer the phone when you're free and let it ring when you're not.

Concerts.
Many bars are equipped with a television set that streams the live performance so that concert goers don't miss anything while replenishing their cocktails. Maybe you can't see the act live, but it's still a free show!

CONS

No Tip Jar.
Very few places have a policy against accepting tips. But how many times have you gone to a baseball game and left the guy five bucks for the five beers you're carting away?

Seasonal.
Despite many men's fantasies, football season doesn't last forever. You'll have a job as long as your team is winning or until the season ends. So check to see if the venue is frequently booked for other events.

PROS	CONS

PROS

Benefits.
Besides a nice insurance package covering health, vision, and dental, you'll receive perks like free meals, reduced hotel rates for friends and family, and discounts at other hotels owned by the same company.

Short Term Relationships.
The couple honeymooning from Oklahoma will become your best friends for four days and then leave just when they start to get annoying.

Advancement.
If you're interested in this industry, it's easy to move up the ladder quickly. Your days are long but you can earn a nice living (and vacation at a discount!).

Day Shift.
As long as it's a destination hotel, you can make a lot of cash bartending during the day. Poolside bars and ocean view lobbies encourage people to get their drink on early.

CONS

Expensive Drinks.
The hotel gains but you lose when people make up for the cost of their drink by slighting your tip.

Missing Customers.
In lobby bars people tend to wander off with their drinks as if the olive has a tracking device. Locating them to pay their tab can be a nightmare.

Travel Dependent.
If the national security level is elevated, the economy's in a slump, or if it's hurricane season, hotel traffic will suffer.

Formalities.
Even if a couple insists that you use their first names, you are still required to address them as Mr. and Mrs. Vacationer. There's an official way to do something from the way you hang a lime to the way you present the bill.

A Bartender's **TIP**

Some hotels offer a one-time "Guest Experience" to all new employees. You choose a night to familiarize yourself with the room service, the spa, and all the amenities of an over-night stay. Ask the hotel you're interested in if it offers this perk. After all, who better to talk up the hot stone massage or beach-side yoga class than the bartender?

ALERT! ALERT!

If your hotel is frequented by a lot of foreigners, find out what the policy is for adding gratuity to the check. Otherwise you'll get stiffed by tourists who aren't accustomed to tipping, or who pretend not to know better.

"A repeat clientele makes you feel like you're going to work to hang out with friends, and they generally keep your tip average high."

GENERAL TIDBITS

Upscale Menus

Higher price points typically draw a more generous clientele. Working in steak or seafood restaurants will drive up your tip.

Full Bars

Beer and wine venues are lovely, and many people will spend a lot on a good bottle of wine. But it's also nice to work at a place that offers a fine, aged scotch.

One Bartender Per Shift

It's great if you have the bar to yourself because then you don't have to split your tips. If there are several bartenders each night, be sure the bar is busy on a regular basis.

Barbacks

A good barback (the guy or gal who is devoted solely to helping you behind the bar) will make or break you. He'll keep your bar continually stocked with clean glasses and fresh condiments, and he'll clear the dirty plates. Make sure your bar has someone designated for this job, and always tip him or her well.

Tip-outs

Tipping the barbacks or bus-boys is a given. But will you also be required to tip out the hostess? The take-out delivery guy? The valet parker? The bouncer? Find out how many people your precious pennies will be going to at the end of each shift.

Busy Streets

A prime location with good parking (self or valet) or convenient public transportation is a plus.

A Bartender's TIP

When you find the place you like, have a drink there on a weekend night and then again on a Monday or Tuesday. Observe the bartender, the drinks she makes, the crowd she serves to, and the overall vibe. If you like what you see, put in your application!

Notes

4

CHAPTER FOUR
GETTING THE JOB

The Resumé

Most of the **smarts** you've acquired at your previous or current job will contribute to your success as a bartender. What are some of the skills your future boss will be looking for on paper?

- Enthusiasm for customer service
- Basic financial knowledge (smarts!)
- Experience in a fast paced environment (speed!)
- Strong work ethic

Look at the resumé that landed you your last job. Switch some of the wording into bar-friendly language that hits the bullets above. Use this example as a guide.

ALERT! ALERT! !!

If you're quietly looking to leave your current job, a reference check to your boss probably won't go over well. Most potential employers understand this dilemma and will respect your request not to call until you've been offered the position. They will however want to call someone else, and they **will** do it. Make sure you have a strong set of past work references.

Misty Smith

1234 Red Robin Road
Little Town, MD 98765

Bank of the United States: Bank Teller
(July '10 – present)

- Provided exceptional customer service for hundreds of clients a day
- Handled cash transitions ranging from small amounts to tens of thousands of dollars
- Communicated regularly with employees from other branches, management, and executives from the regional office

Green Road Elementary School: 3rd Grade Teacher
(Sept '07 – June '09)

- Exceptional classroom management skills and conflict resolution training
- Created, organized, and implemented original lesson plans for over 70 students
- Trained in facilitating student to student peer mediation sessions
- Led the school & community campus beautification project, involving over 50 volunteers and a $10,000 budget

Quick Cuisine Catering: Server and Bartender
(Oct '09 – present)

- Bartended at private parties and special events ranging from birthdays to corporate functions
- Continually adapted to new bar set-ups with a minimum of cocktail-making equipment available
- Performed a variety of roles depending on the need, such as bartender, waitress, expeditor, barback, clean-up crew, etc.

The Retro Retail Store: Sales
(Summers from 2000 – '06)

- Responsible for managing and maintaining a large inventory of clothing and accessories
- Selected for the Key Keepers Club for the continual balance of my registers
- Met or exceeded the daily sales goal 92% of the time

The Dress

Let your personality show your **sass**. Keep your outfit respectable whether you're applying for a bartending job at a bowling alley or a night club. Just because the women where you'd like to work strut around in Daisy Dukes and leopard print heels, doesn't mean you should dress like that for your interview.

Here are a few suggestions to make that dreaded closet search easier:

Independent Bar/ Restaurant:

Casual Nice
- Dark jeans, khakis, blouse, sweater, long-sleeved shirt
- Flats, low heels, dress shoes

Chain Restaurant:

Business Casual, Conservative
- Dark jeans, knee-length skirt, slacks, blouse, sweater
- Flats, low heels, dress shoes

Night Club

Sexy Classy
- Anything black, form-fitting shirt and skirt or pants
- Flats, low or high heels, high boots

Hotel Bar:

Classy and Conservative
- Blouse and slacks or knee-length skirt, suit, dress
- Dress shoes, low heels

ALERT! ALERT! !!

Never wear tank tops, flip flops, or midriff revealing shirts…even if you're applying for beach side bartending on a private tropical island. Your interview is your chance to show your professionalism, classiness, and common sense. Dress to impress and leave the comfort at home.

Notes

5

CHAPTER FIVE
YOUR FIRST DAY OF WORK

You've scouted the ideal bar, interviewed with a fabulous resumé and the perfect outfit, and got the job. You're in! To keep it, here are some things to remember:

Arrive Early

Check with your boss to see if you can come in extra early on your first day. Even a veteran bartender will be slowed down if she doesn't know where to reach for the tequila or bourbon. Most bars have what is called a Speed Bar. A Speed Bar is arranged just below the ledge of the bar for easy access for the bartender. It usually includes these frequently used spirits: vodka, gin, tequila, bourbon, rum, and triple sec.

Make Nice

Introduce yourself to everyone who works in the place, most importantly the busboys or barbacks. These guys will continually pack your ice bin, replenish your garnish tray, and stock your glasses.

Learn the other bartenders and waiters' names. You'll be asking for their help all night and "Yo bitch, c'mere" might not go over well.

Good Questions

If a question about the computer system comes up, don't hesitate to call for help. Hitting too many of the wrong buttons in a row can cause major problems for you at the end of the night.

Be aggressive about introducing yourself to regulars and asking for names.

Find out what the protocol is for a power outage. If the business accepts credit cards, you'll need a backup plan when the computer system goes down.

If a customer needs to know the ingredients of a menu item for dietary reasons or just plain curiosity, get her an answer. Chances are you'll get that same question a hundred times, and you never want to guess or give the wrong answer.

Ask for ID if you have the slightest suspicion that someone might not be of age. No one will ever be offended for asking if she is under 21.

Bad Questions

Don't ask to have the 4th of July off, or any other holiday for that matter until you've been there for a while and earned some seniority. If there is an important date coming up that you must have off, bring it up during your interview.

Don't ask when you can clock out. Your boss will let you know when it's time to go.

Don't ask when you'll get to work Fridays and Saturdays. You'll get there in a few months when someone else leaves, or in a few weeks when your speed and sass are clearly boosting your boss' bottom line.

A Bartender's TIP

At a new job, I always keep a little notepad and pencil next to the register with a diagram of the bar. I write down each customer's name and drink. If you're able to say "Bye Steve and Harry" as they leave, you'll score a few points and maybe a regular.

Be An Actress

Despite your preparation, there's bound to be a drink that stumps you. Here are some responses to have ready:

"You know, I haven't made one of those in a while…remind me how it's done."

"I can make that a couple different ways. How do you like it?"

"There's a classic recipe I've been meaning to try. Let me look it up."

ALERT! ALERT!

In some states, if a person forgets her ID you can verbally ask her if she's over 21 and be cleared of any possible lawsuits. But this is really risky and not as fail-proof as checking the real thing.

Drink Advice

People will always want to know what you recommend. Have a couple suggestions ready.

sweet drink
Bay Breeze
Cosmo
Mai Tai

sour drink
Lemon Drop
Midori Sour
Side Car

strong drink
Manhattan
Long Island
Wild Turkey & Soda

mild drink
Cape Cod
Strawberry Daiquiri
Tom Collins

tropical drink
Planter's Punch
Piña Colada
Sex on the Beach

CHAPTER SIX
SAFETY AND THE LAW

You can't serve alcohol without understanding the consequences of serving a person too much. The blood-alcohol level that qualifies a person as legally intoxicated is determined by individual states and localities. What does it come down to? Don't over-serve. If you realize that a person has had too much to drink, make certain that he or she is being driven home by a friend or taking a cab (more on this below).

Rate of Alcohol Absorption

There are many factors to consider when determining the rate at which a person can become intoxicated. The first is weight.

If Maria, who weighs 100 pounds, drinks a glass of wine quickly, she may not be sober enough to operate a hair dryer. But Debbie, a 300-pound goddess of a woman, might drink a glass of wine in the same amount of time and not only be able to use the hair dryer, but re-assemble it into a remote-control airplane.

However, if Debbie the Goddess skipped breakfast, takes three medications not compatible with alcohol, and is drinking by the pool on a blistering summer day, she may pass out cold in the cabaña after only three sips of wine.

The real key is time. If Maria wants to finish a bottle of wine on her own and still drive home, she better do so over a twelve-hour period with lots of snacking along the way.

Below is the **Blood Alcohol Concentration Chart (BAC)** for California. Use this as a reference; however, check your state's specific guidelines.

TIME FROM FIRST DRINK	90 – 109 lbs. TOTAL DRINKS								110 – 129 lbs. TOTAL DRINKS								130 – 149 lbs. TOTAL DRINKS								150 – 169 lbs. TOTAL DRINKS							
	1	2	3	4	5	6	7	8	1	2	3	4	5	6	7	8	1	2	3	4	5	6	7	8	1	2	3	4	5	6	7	8
1 HOUR																																
2 HOURS																																
3 HOURS																																
4 HOURS																																

TIME FROM FIRST DRINK	170 – 189 lbs. TOTAL DRINKS								190 – 209 lbs. TOTAL DRINKS								209 lbs. & UP TOTAL DRINKS							
	1	2	3	4	5	6	7	8	1	2	3	4	5	6	7	8	1	2	3	4	5	6	7	8
1 HOUR																								
2 HOURS																								
3 HOURS																								
4 HOURS																								

KEY	
.01% – .04%	POSSIBLE DUI
.05% – .07%	LIKELY DUI
.05% – .07%	DEFINITELY DUI

Fatty Foods & Coffee

You've seen it a hundred times in the movies. A guy with one eye barely open sits slouched over his drink in an empty bar. Joe, the concerned bartender, gently pushes the cocktail away and sets down a steaming cup of coffee. "Here Jimmy, better drink this." Jimmy has a few sips and is suddenly coherent and alert, ready to carry on as the decisive, wise hero that he is.

Back in the real world, a cup of coffee that's strong enough to hold up a pitch-fork won't make you any less drunk. It's a total myth. Caffeine may turn a drunk into a hyper-active drunk (ever ordered a vodka with Red Bull?), but by no means does it qualify a person to get behind the wheel of a car. And sucking down a bucket of water may do wonders for that nasty hangover come morning, but it won't dry a person up any sooner.

If you want to retard the speed at which alcohol affects the body, offer foods high in fat. Nuts, French fries, cheese, and ice cream are all good options. But again, this won't make a person sober, it will just prolong the process of becoming drunk.

PERSONAL STORY: Sara

Once in a while I'll order a plate of onion rings or French fries on the house for a couple that's getting a little tipsy. So as not to embarrass anyone, I just tell them that I made a mistake and I don't want the food to go to waste. I set it down and walk away so they can't refuse it. This doesn't mean I'll let them get behind the wheel if I think one of them can't drive. But if their drinks are half full and they'll be around a while, it helps slow things down.

The Placebo Effect

There may be occasions to cut someone off without necessarily making it obvious. This is when using what I call a "placebo" comes in handy. A placebo can be appropriate for the birthday boy who has been drinking since he rolled out of bed, or the over-served bride-to-be during the bachelorette outing. At any point in the evening his or her drunkenness may be way ahead of the rest of the party's. If some unsolicited help is needed for slowing things down, you might start pouring half the amount of alcohol, or none at all. Most likely it won't even be noticed. Just remember these important guidelines:

○ If you pour less than the regular amount of alcohol, you shouldn't charge the regular price of the drink.

○ When you completely omit the alcohol, it's officially a virgin drink and should be billed as such.

○ If possible, include the friends of the-life-of-the-party in the drink selection. They know their friend best and may just prescribe a glass of water.

○ If the customer is dining alone and becoming tipsy, let him or her know that it's time to pay up and call a cab, or switch to a mocktail.

Safety Tips

It goes without saying that you should be on guard any time you leave a bar late at night. But since you'll usually be the one locking up, here are some safety tips to keep in mind:

Never close up shop by yourself or leave with just one other woman. Three's a good crowd, especially if there's a man in the mix. It's smart to make a busboy stay on the clock while you wrap things up.

Always have a male staff member walk you to your car if it's dark. You're carrying a lot of tips in cash and you don't need to risk your safety (or rent money).

If someone gives you the creeps, trust your instincts, and try to get rid of him well before closing.

The police are just a phone call away. Have the non-emergency number next to the phone in case it looks like there'll be a situation.

If someone walks in who looks like he's in need of restraints and padded walls, tell him the place has been rented out for a private party and to come back another time.

Some Serious Stuff

If you serve drinks to someone who then gets into a car and subsequently into an accident, the driver, the passengers, or the victims can sue you and the establishment you work at. So be careful. You want people to have a good time, but you also have a responsibility to cut someone off when he or she has had too much.

A Bartender's TIP

Don't be afraid to turn a customer away if you think she's already loaded. Simply say you aren't comfortable serving her and that she should come back another time. If she throws a fit, you know you've made the right decision.

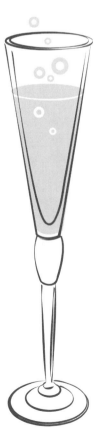

7

CHAPTER SEVEN
THINGS TO KNOW ABOUT WINE AND LIQUOR

You could fill a department store with the number of books written on beer, wine, and spirits. But what you actually need to know to get a bartending job can fit onto an index card. Take a quick quiz to see where you fall on the drink IQ barometer. You probably already know a lot more than you realize.

1. An aperitif is:

a) A rare parrot found in the Amazon

b) A before dinner drink

c) Another name for a brooch that your grandmother might wear

d) A special glass for serving rum

2. The difference between sherry and brandy is:

a) Brandy is made from distilling wine and sherry is a fortified wine

b) Sherry is a blonde and brandy is a red head

c) One should be served in a coconut and the other should be consumed straight from the bottle

d) Sherry is burgundy and brandy is clear

3. Vodka comes from:

a) Food plants such as barley, wheat, rye, and potato

b) A natural spring that runs beneath Russia

c) Vodka trees

d) White leafy vegetables processed through coal

4. The difference between "well" and "call" liquor is:

a) You'll either feel well enough to swing from the chandeliers, or need to call for the doctor

b) One comes from a well in the earth deep below the bar and the other is delivered after you call an alcohol service

c) Well liquor is the least expensive brand. Call is anything above that, often the best of what the bar has to offer

d) Well liquor is exclusively made in the US but call liquor is only brewed on foreign soil

5. Tequila is made from:

a) Agave plants

b) Marinating Tunilla Cactus leaves

c) Collecting rain drops after tropical storms

d) Drilling a hole into the center of ancient Mexican rocks

6. The difference between bourbon and whiskey is:

a) Bourbon makes you smell like a cowboy and whiskey makes you yelp like one

b) Both come from grains but one is made from at least 51% corn

c) Bourbon should only be enjoyed while watching Tennessee Williams movies. Whiskey goes best with Soaps

d) There is no difference. Unless it is actually made in the city of bourbon, Tennessee, it must be given another name

7. Pinot Noir and Pinot Grigio are different because:

a) One comes from a red grape and the other comes from a white grape

b) Pinot Noir is a dinner wine and Pinot Grigio is served with lunch

c) The Pinot family named Noir after their son, and Grigio after their daughter

d) One is flat and the other is sparkling

8. Beer is made by:

a) Your refrigerator

b) The NFL

c) Reducing grains like oats, barley, and corn into a malt

d) Churning wheat in a barrel with pebbles until a fine amber liquid develops

9. Champagne is different from sparkling wine because:

a) There is no difference between the two

b) Sparkling wine is easy to pronounce whereas some people accidentally refer to the other as Sham-pag-knee

c) Champagne is always super expensive and sparkling wine is dirt cheap

d) No vineyards outside of Champagne, France are legally allowed to produce it and give it the name Champagne

10. The difference between a bartender and a mixologist is (trick question!):

a) Bartenders work in bars and mixologists work in labs

b) A bartender simply follows directions from a recipe book whereas a mixologist never pours the same drink twice

c) You're a bartender until you retire. After that you're considered a mixologist

d) There is no clear difference; both terms are open to one's personal interpretation

Easy quiz, right? Now pour a glass of wine and take a sip for every right answer (for wrong answers take two sips!)

1. B

An aperitif is a before dinner drink and ranges from a martini to a beer. It's the drink people have at the bar before sitting down for dinner.

2. A

Sherry and brandy are wines enjoyed before dinner as an aperitif or as a drinkable dessert. Sherry is a dryer wine (meaning less sugar) until fortified with brandy to make it sweeter. Brandy, which comes from the Dutch word "brandewijn" and means "burnt wine," is made by distilling wine and then aging it, usually in oak barrels. Familiarize yourself with the brandy rating system:

A.C.
Aged 2 years in wood

V.S.
"Very Special," aged at least 3 years in wood

V.S.O.P.
"Very Superior Old Pale," aged at least 5 years in wood

X.O.
"Extra Old," aged at least 6 years

3. A

Vodka comes from a variety of grains like barley, wheat, and rye. Over the years, companies have become more creative and make vodka from things like quinoa and rice. It doesn't always tell you on the bottle but the original packaging will specify the source of the vodka.

4. C

Well liquor is used when someone doesn't specify a brand name for his or her beverage. For example, if a customer asks for a vodka tonic instead of a Kettle or Belvedere and tonic, you will pour from the row of bottles your employer has designated for all standard recipes. Well liquor usually costs less than the premium brands, otherwise known as the call liquor. Call liquor should really only be used upon request, and not as a tool to push up the price of a drink. However, many high-end bars and five star hotels carry only premium spirits for well drinks, and there's no reason the customer needs to know the price unless he asks for it.

ALERT! ALERT!

A lot of bars want you to up-sell every order. If a customer requests a gin & tonic, your boss may require you to offer Tanqueray or Sapphire instead of simply pouring the well. Find out what the policy is. We happen to find up-selling offensive. If a person wants a premium alcohol, he'll ask for it. Don't make him feel cheap.

5. A

The Agave plant supplies the wonderful taste of tequila. The juice from the heart of it is fermented and distilled. Golden tequilas get their wonderful color after aging for a few years in oak barrels, much like wine.

6. B

Bourbon and whiskey are so similar that most people will order by brand. What you should know is that every bourbon is a whiskey but not every whiskey is bourbon. A genuine bourbon can only be made in the USA. Both are made from ingredients such as barley, rye, wheat, and corn. The important difference is that bourbon is made from a minimum of 51% corn, and should be at least 80 proof. Not all whiskeys have to be aged (bourbon does for at least two years) and can be made from many different types of grain.

7. A

Pinot Noir is a red wine and Pinot Grigio is a white. If you are new to wines, these can be just as hard to keep straight as Cabernet Sauvignon and Sauvignon Blanc. Most people will simply toss out "Pinot" and "Cab" when they want the red. For the whites customers tend to say "Pinot Grigio" in its entirety, but just Sauvignon for the white. If your boss will allow it (and a smart one will), have a taste of each wine sometime during your first week. It will help you remember the difference and allow you to offer your honest opinion when asked (because you'll be asked a lot).

PERSONAL STORY: *Torey*

At my bar, the house Chardonnay is one of our best, and the house Merlot one of our worst. I'm never afraid to tell customers what I think and they are always very appreciative. You can also offer a little taste of a few wines if someone is having a hard time making up her mind. People usually show their appreciation for this in the tip.

8. C

Beer is one of the biggest sellers in any bar and the easiest "drink" you'll ever make. The brewing process for beer is taken very seriously, and may vary from one brewery to the next. Microbreweries or craft breweries are creating beers with non-traditional ingredients, and gaining large followings. Familiarize yourself with which beers in your bar are dark, light, pale, amber, "lite," etc. And if your bar offers beer on tap, make sure that you or one of the barbacks knows how to change the keg quickly when it's out.

9. D

Champagne is a sparkling wine, but only sparkling wine made in Champagne, France, can officially bear the name "Champagne." There are very strict rules regarding the viticulture of Champagne, and if the guidelines aren't followed, the Comité Interprofessionel du Vin de Champagne can step in and take legal action. Any beverage similar to champagne but made outside of that particular region, is referred to as sparkling wine. Just like with champagne, the price and quality will vary.

10. D

Everyone will have a different answer about mixology. This Girl's opinion is that a bartender will always be considered a mixologist but a mixologist may not always be considered a bartender. Bartenders mix drinks all night long. Sometimes the mixing will involve a new creation, other times it will be for an old classic, but they are doing everything I consider to be mixology. On the other hand, a person can design the most imaginative new drinks at home but with no audience and no tips, this mixologist isn't really a bartender.

8

CHAPTER EIGHT
TERMINOLOGY AND SERVING TIPS

What does that mean?

Expression	Meaning
On the Rocks	Pour my drink over ice
Neat	No ice in my drink, please
Up	Shake it with ice, then strain it into a martini glass
Stirred	Gently stir the ingredients in the shaker with ice with a spoon or swirl the shaker with your hand
Shaken, Not Stirred	Shake the drink as opposed to stirring it. (Unless requested, you'll always shake it. This order usually comes from a James Bond wannabe who simply wants to utter those famous words out loud)
Coke Back	I want my Coke on the side instead of in my drink (don't charge extra)
Beer Back	Along with my drink (usually a shot), I'd like a beer (which you do charge for)
Black and Blue	Shake my drink like you're kicking the shit outta the kid who tormented you in junior high
Easy Ice / Juice / Soda	Don't put too much ice in my drink (In other words, make it strong)
Chilled	Make my drink cold without using ice
Heated	Make my drink warm (see diagram)

FOLLOW THESE STEPS FOR WARMING A DRINK.

Fill the cognac glass with hot water. Repeat if necessary until the glass is warm when empty.

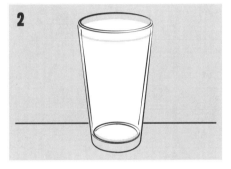

Fill a pint glass or a martini shaker with hot water. Place it on a towel to absorb any overflow once the cognac glass is put into position.

Pour the cognac into the warmed snifter, and carefully place the snifter into the hot water. Leave the glass for a few minutes to allow for the cognac to heat through.

Remove the snifter from the hot water, wipe any excess water from the exterior of the glass, and serve.

Most customers are happy to wait for this extra service, so don't rush it. I always did it when I had time, even when people didn't ask. It's a really nice touch and brings you a few extra bucks in the tip. Never microwave it, or ask the kitchen to warm the liquor in a pan. Too much of the alcohol evaporates, and you never know if the kitchen staff scrubbed all the fish odor out of the pan.

CHAPTER NINE
BAR ETIQUETTE

You can guess some of the obvious rules of bartending:

Don't clear a cocktail before it's empty, or set a drink down by the rim, or flirt with a married man when his wife is sitting right next to him. But understanding the unspoken rules will save you from embarrassment and help you keep your job.

Free Drinks

Your boss will tell you never to pour a free drink because all the profit is in the liquor. But to not buy the occasional cocktail can be very insulting. Use your judgment and don't risk your job over a drink. Give out the comps as infrequently as possible and definitely not during your first six months on the job.

Here are the exceptions for breaking your boss's rule:

○ Bob the banker stops in four times a week for his Bookers on the rocks. He always has a few drinks and never tips you less than 20%. Every so often, after he has ordered his second drink, set it down and say, "This one's on the house."

○ If there's a regular who drinks wine, don't be afraid to top it off every now and then.

○ A group of, say, seven or more comes in late one night to celebrate a birthday. If it looks like they are only going to have one round, let 'em pay. But if they have several, go ahead and buy the birthday boy a drink.

○ If one of your besties drops by now and then, don't even think about letting her pay. But if Natasha's sister's best friend from the holistic detox weekend retreat comes in and expects to rehydrate at the bar's expense, then deliver her bill without hesitation.

When not to give freebies:

○ If your friends show up expecting to indulge in an all-you-can-drink-buffet. Feel awkward handing them a check? Then pay for their drinks out of your own pocket.

○ If someone asks for it. This major faux pas deserves a hasty bill. We'd even consider charging them twice.

○ If they expect it. See above.

○ If something is wrong with the guest's meal. Call the manager over and replace the food, or take it off his or her check. Your boss would rather lose money on the coq au vin than on a cocktail.

Staff Meals & Drinks

- Find out from a co-worker what the policy is on drinking (asking the boss gives the wrong vibe). Many places will allow the staff to drink at half price, but only after their shift is over and they have changed out of uniform.

- You'd be surprised how many people will offer to buy you a drink. Sometimes it's to show off, but usually it's a form of appreciation (or a plan to up the chances of getting your number). Accepting it builds good rapport. If it's not the right time to drink it, accept their offer and tell them you'll be enjoying it at the end of your shift.

- A lot of restaurants offer a shift meal. The kitchen will either make food specifically for the staff, or you'll get to sample the specials that will be offered that night. You may also get an employee discount on food (go easy on the chocolate cake).

- In some states, the law requires you to take a break. Fat chance you'll get one. And even if you did take 15, you try telling 40 thirsty customers to hold on while you eat your peanut butter and jelly sandwich. Bring an energy bar to snack on if there's a lull.

- If you do have time to eat during your shift, find a private spot to enjoy your food. The customer will be hesitant to ask for a drink refill or a new napkin if you're in the middle of dinner.

- The rumors you've heard about high traces of urine in the bar nuts are true. Even if you are starving, don't eat them unless they are straight from the jar. We've seen dozens of people slobber all over their fingers and then stick them right back into the nut bowl. No, thank you.

86ing – 2 meanings

When the kitchen runs out of an item, the chef will say something like, "The risotto is 86'd," or "86 the lasagna!" Customers get pretty upset when they've put in an order only to be told 20 minutes later that it's no longer available. A good kitchen staff will alert the servers at the beginning of the night to just how many crab legs or ribeyes are in stock.

"86'd" is also the curse-free way of telling a customer he's not welcome anymore. "86ing" might happen if:

- Some bloke comes in drunk and won't leave quietly when you refuse to serve him.

- While dining, a customer becomes hostile, belligerent, verbally aggressive, or starts harassing people.

- Some cheap chump refuses to pay and attempts to walk out.

- That jackass at table 4 becomes even more of a jackass.

PERSONAL STORY: Megan

I remember one Christmas Eve this guy sat down at the bar who gave me the creeps. When he ordered, I was rude. Then, being that it was Christmas, I started feeling guilty, thinking, "Come on, it's the holidays after all and this lonely guy just wants a nice meal. Don't be a bitch." Just then, a waitress called me over and said that two years ago there was an employee whom he stalked. The girl eventually filed a restraining order. Just as I was figuring out how to tell a sober customer that he would be 86'd for something that happened two years ago, he put down some cash and left. I was relieved to be spared that particular 86ing and even happier that I never saw him again.

Dating

Because you're the sexy sassy woman you are, you probably get asked out on dates whether you're at the club or the dry cleaners. Well guess what, it's also going to happen at work when you're behind the bar. Just remember this: you make the bed you lie in. Be careful when dating a customer or a colleague. Your place of work is sacred, and if things go south, you don't want to be reminded of your mistake every time you report for duty.

○ Here are some tips for graciously handling yourself when you're on the spot **and** on center stage.

○ Even if you're married, a guy won't always take note of your ring finger before asking you out, regardless of the size of your diamonds. If you're engaged or married, let the poor guy down easy by saying you're flattered, but taken.

○ Some chaps' egos are more fragile than others. Have a couple of prepared statements for declining a date (they don't have to be true). For example, "Thank you but I'm actually in a relationship," or "You're sweet, but I'm just getting over a rough break-up," or even, "My therapist insists that I let the meds kick in and that I end my stuffed animal collection before I get married again."

○ Then there's always the "wedding ring fake-out," which will deter many. Buy a cheap, fake diamond ring and convince even yourself that your wedding cake was picture perfect. This will allow you to be as flirty as you need to be without anyone getting his hopes up.

○ If you do want to accept an offer for a night out on the town, always have him give you his number for these reasons:

You don't have time! You're working!

There might be some creep-o who catches a glimpse of your number if your suitor leaves it out too long.

Maybe you'll call him tomorrow, maybe you won't. It's good to be in control of your dating schedule.

> **PERSONAL STORY:** *Leigh*
>
> A waitress I worked with dated a regular for a while. After their bad breakup, he wasn't willing to find a new place to drink and she wasn't going to find a new place to work. Every time he came in we jumped through hoops to make sure they never saw each other. It was difficult to say the least.

Conversations

○ **Mind your own business.** One of the true skills of a bartender is knowing when to participate in a conversation and when to just eavesdrop. Stay out of it unless you are obviously being included.

○ **Don't react.** For some mysterious reason people think that there's a sound-proof barrier between their bar stool and you. Men will go into detail, and we mean detail, about the women they bring home. Women will disclose their latest adventure in plastic surgery, all while you stand inches away. They don't think you can hear them, so don't act like you can. You'll be both shocked and thoroughly entertained.

Tipping Out

○ Every bar has a different policy, so ask about the tip-out amount right away. Customarily you give out 10% of your total tips to the busboys or barbacks (it's split between them).

○ Sometimes the hostess is tipped out, but this varies from bar to bar.

○ An especially nice perk of working in a restaurant is getting tipped out from the servers. Depending on the place, they'll either give you 10% of their total tips, or 10% of their beverage sales gross.

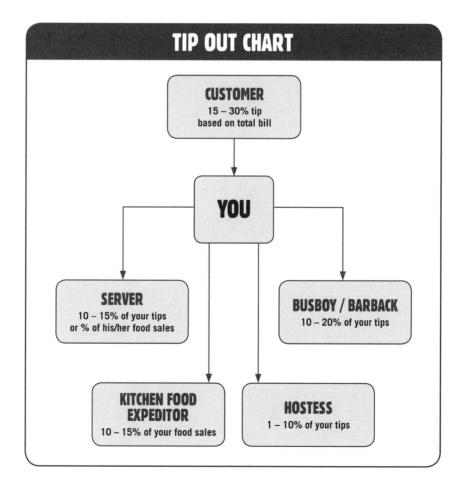

TIP OUT CHART

CUSTOMER
15 – 30% tip
based on total bill

YOU

SERVER
10 – 15% of your tips
or % of his/her food sales

BUSBOY / BARBACK
10 – 20% of your tips

KITCHEN FOOD EXPEDITOR
10 – 15% of your food sales

HOSTESS
1 – 10% of your tips

10

CHAPTER TEN
DEALING WITH DRUNKS

Not all lushes are created equal, so you gotta know how to deal with each type on an individual basis. Here are the 10 we've encountered the most and some advice on how to respond to their "entertaining" behavior.

1. The Love Bird

Warning Signs:
Gets increasingly googly-eyed at anything that moves as the night goes on. This includes strangers, bartenders, busboys, and barstools.

Heard Saying:
"Was your father a thief? Because I think he stole the moon and put it in your eyes."

What We've Witnessed:
A man and woman who were complete strangers at the beginning of the night, and practically procreating by closing.

How to Deal:
Be grateful if the Love Bird remains fully clothed and try not to vomit in your mouth at the one-liners.

2. The Egomaniac Slime Bucket

Warning Signs:
Speaks loudly, brags unabashedly, and buys drinks for everyone at the bar whenever he senses his limelight fading.

Heard Shouting:
"This weekend I think I'll fly my plane to the lake-house and just chill with a couple friends. Unless of course you'd like to come?"

What We've Witnessed:
An Egotistical Slime Bucket regular who tried to put potential dates at ease by insinuating he'd slept with a few of the waitresses.

How to Deal:
Ignoring them works best and drives them nuts.

3. The Introspective Drunk

Warning Signs:
Takes 30 minutes to find a drink that matches her mood.

Heard Saying:
"I think I feel like drinking something gentle."

What We've Witnessed:
A guy who journaled for three hours on half a stack of paper bar napkins.

How to Deal:
As long as he keeps drinking, let him be. This type of drunk is usually low maintenance and easy to please.

4. The Pig

Warning Signs:
Leaves food clumps along the rim of his cocktail glass.

Heard Saying:
"Cook my fries so well done that there's no potato left in the middle."

What We've Witnessed:
A man who stuffed himself so full of food and liquor that he vomited all over the bar and his friend.

How to Deal:
Have a pair of latex gloves and bleach (and maybe a hazmat suit) ready for the clean-up.

5. The Drunk Drunk

Warning Signs:
Staggers into the bar intoxicated and orders a double shot of whatever you happen to be pouring.

Heard Saying:
"I was driving home when I realized I forgot to get one for the road."

What We've Witnessed:
A man fall off his barstool, bust his chin open (7 stitches), and return for more drinks the same night.

How to Deal:
If you think he's drunk when he arrives, don't serve him anything with liquor. Offer a seat, a glass of water, and a cab ride home.

6. Ms. / Mr. Personality

Warning Signs:
Sits down and immediately joins a stranger's conversation. Wants to know everyone's first name and uses it repetitively to an uncomfortable degree.

Heard Saying:
"Let's shut this place down and take the party to our house!"

What We've Witnessed:
A couple who wiggled their way into receiving a wedding invitation from the couple they just met.

How to Deal:
Be grateful that someone other than you is entertaining the customers.

7. The Exhibitionist

Warning Signs:
Provocative clothing, excessive breasts, pecs, or arm muscles. Chooses a barstool visible to the most people in the room.

Heard Saying:
"You should see the size of my ----!"

What We've Witnessed:
A man who called a waitress over to ask for change, and had the hundred dollar bill on his thigh, right next to his exposed you-know-what.

How to Deal:
When there are bare body parts involved, phone the police or the nearest psycho ward.

8. The Depressed Drunk

Warning Signs:
Crying, moping, whining, extreme self-deprecation.

Heard Saying:
They don't say much actually. They just sit there and act, well...depressed.

What We've Witnessed:
A guy break down for no reason and totally start to sob. The rest of the bar got so quiet you could hear an ice cube melt.

How to Deal:
Just pour the drink and try not to let it get you down!

9. The Angry Drunk

Warning Signs:
Gets annoyed if you don't make his drink in a nano-second.

Heard Saying:
"I'm one fucking angry drunk!"

What We've Witnessed:
Walls punched, salt-shakers smashed, martini glasses thrown.

How to Deal:
Under-serve, stay clear, and call the bouncer.

10. The My-Life-Is-Better-Than-Yours-Drunk

Warning Signs:
Asks WAY too many personal questions.

Heard Saying:
"You could do a lot more with your life, you know."

What We've Witnessed:
A bartender run to the liquor closet in tears after being told she wasn't living up to her potential.

How to Deal:
The people who judge your life are usually the biggest losers in the world. So try a statement like, "You inspire me. Really. You come in every night and drink and drink and drink. If I can live up to your high standard? to your incredible potential? then I will really truly have made something of myself."

Notes

11

CHAPTER ELEVEN
MONEY MANAGEMENT

With money piling up before your eyes, you may be tempted to replace your entire wardrobe with Marc Jacobs, or fund a weekend trip to Vegas for the girls. Before you do, use your smarts to plan for your future. Retirement may seem a long way away, but it's never too soon to start putting those pennies in the bank. Once you've hit your savings goal each month, you can indulge in those shopping sprees and get-aways.

High Interest Savings Account:

Financial experts agree that you should have three months of living expenses available in cash. If that seems overwhelming, shoot for one month. You never know when a slow month might hit, or the unexpected car repair.

Traditional IRA:

If each year you can contribute up to $4,000 into your IRA, then that's about $340 a month, or $30 a shift (if you work three times a week). Because of compound interest, you'll be sitting pretty when you decide to retire.

Stock Market:

With all the user-friendly financial websites available today, investing has become accessible to everyone. We recommend getting guidance with this type of venture, but there are ways to make money in the short term and long term.

Real Estate:

Buying a home may feel like it's decades away. But the money you're setting aside every night will add up quickly. A one-bedroom condo in your neighborhood may be more affordable than you think.

Small Business:

Find other ways for your hard-earned money to make more hard-earned money. Open a CD at your bank. Make greeting cards to sell to local gift shops. Buy a row of gum-ball machines for the market down the street. Sell your unwanted Christmas gifts on ebay. Be creative!

PERSONAL STORY: *Janice*

On an exceptionally busy night, one of the waitresses gave me $50 at tip-out, which meant she had made $500. The next night she came in complaining of how broke she was. Jokingly I asked her what happened to all her money. She didn't answer but held up a bulging shopping bag.

Sample Budget

TAKE HOME TIPS: $300

1
PAY YOURSELF

5 – 10% of income ($5 – $30) into:

Traditional IRA

401(k)

High Interest Savings Account

2
PAY FIXED EXPENSES

Rent

Utilities

Transportation Costs

Groceries

3
FLEXIBLE INCOME

Meals Out

Shopping Sprees

Weekend Excursions

Notes

....

....

....

....

....

....

12

CHAPTER TWELVE
THE 3-DAY CRAM

This Chapter is designed for the person who wants to land a bartending job within a few days.

Maybe you'd like to supplement your income with a second job or just need a valid reason to quit your current position. Our study and practice schedule might be reminiscent of any school or work project that you ever put off to the last minute, requiring extra focus and commitment. However, it's completely accomplishable and perfect for those who need a job like, yesterday.

Clear your calendar, roll up your sleeves, and follow our step-by-step instructions for a crash course in bartending.

Day 1

○ Purchase your copy of **This Girl Walks Into A Bar.**

○ Curl up on the couch with a glass of wine or a cup of tea and read the book through to get the gist. Be sure to cover all the drink recipes too.

○ Your first priority will be to memorize and practice the fifteen drinks of the TOP 15. These are the fifteen cocktails we determined to be the most commonly requested drinks that do not include the ingredients in their names. For example, a vodka tonic, gin and soda, bourbon and Coke, or whiskey sour will be ordered 50% of the time and list all the ingredients in their names. No need for memorization on your part. Hooray! Simply grab a bottle of vodka, add tonic, and voila! The drinks from our TOP 15, however, will require some prior knowledge to make your customer happy.

Day 2

Step One

○ Study the flash cards for the TOP 15 drinks. Focus on the "free pour" measurements because it's easier to switch to a jigger once you get the job rather than the other way around. Make notes or create mnemonic devices on the cards if it will help you remember.

○ Watch some videos on the Internet of bartenders making drinks. Don't be intimidated by bottle juggling or lighting drinks on fire. Unless you're part of a burlesque or circus act, it's unlikely to be part of the job requirement.

○ Get hold of two liquor bottles, preferably empty ones so that you don't waste alcohol. The purpose of this exercise isn't to make the perfect drink but to get used to handling two bottles at one time and filling drinks to the rim. If you have a couple of old bottles at home, pour the contents out and set them aside until after your "cram." If you don't have any, and you've already asked your friends and neighbors for any empty or nearly empty bottles in their cabinet, go to a liquor store or supermarket and purchase two bottles of the cheapest spirits or wine you can find.

○ Pick up a package of pour spouts, a martini shaker, and a strainer.

○ Buy or borrow two or three martini glasses. You'll need practice straining martini drinks right to the rim. Cocktails that require glasses like lowballs, highballs, rocks, and buckets can be improvised since you layer the ingredients in the glass, stir, and serve.

○ Buy 20 lemons, 40 limes, two large cartons of inexpensive juice (your choice) and a large bag of ice.

Step Two

○ When you return home with your supplies, take time to study your flash cards. Visualize the drink as you read each recipe.

○ Grab your cutting board, and take out 20 limes and 10 lemons. Follow our simple diagram on page 96 to learn how to cut wedges and twists. Don't worry if the first few turn out jagged or lopsided. You'll get better as you go along. The goal is to look like you've been doing this for years by cutting and twisting accurately and quickly.

○ Begin your home lesson with the vodka martini, using water as a temporary substitute for vodka.

○ Fill a liquor bottle with water and attach a pour spout.

○ Fill the shaker 2/3 full of ice.

○ Pour in 4 counts (one one-thousand, two one-thousand…) of water into the shaker.

○ Shake the ice and water hard for a few seconds and then strain it into the glass. It should look foggy and have a few ice crystals floating on the surface.

○ Practice making this "drink" over and over until you get your count right and can fill the glass to the rim every time.

○ If you have more than one martini glass, practice doubling, then tripling this recipe by increasing your counts until you pour the right amount in each glass every time.

○ If you only have one martini glass to work with, dump the single glass out and continue emptying the water from the shaker until you are neither short nor over on the second or third pour.

A Bartender's **TIP**

Hold the liquor bottles by the neck, not the bodies, and lift your hand slightly into the air as you pour.

○ Continue making the drinks that
involve a martini glass. Don't worry
about needing triple sec, sweet n' sour,
or sodas. Use whatever juice you have
on hand and imagine the liquor bottles
are filled with the recipe's required
spirit. Your cosmo may look orange
(if you're using orange juice) or white
(if you're using milk), but it doesn't
matter. Just keep getting the feel for
the pour counts.

○ Practice doubling, then tripling these
recipes by increasing your counts
until you pour the right amount in
each glass every time.

○ Move on to drinks that will be served in
a regular cocktail glass, often referred
to as buckets or double old-fashioneds.

○ Line up the glasses and fill them with
ice. Pour in the water, then the juice,
then the mixer, etc. Treat the row of
drinks like an assembly line. Practice
making two, three, four at a time,
and don't forget the lime or lemon
garnish. Practice adding salt to the
rim of the glasses.

○ Continue using alcohol substitutes
until you are comfortable with your
counts and handling the bottles.

Step Three

○ Now it's time for some observation work!
Early enough in the evening to get a
good seat, go to a bar that gets busy
and prepare to take lots of mental notes.
Order a drink from the TOP 15 and
nurse it to buy yourself time. For your
second drink order something different
from the TOP 15. Just be sure to stick
to the same alcohol family if your tummy
is sensitive to switching from one spirit
to another.

Pay attention to:

How the bartender grabs the liquor.

How she has organized the alcohol
in the Speed Bar.

How she uses a Speed Bar or survives
without one.

What types of drinks she's making.

How she handles customers, both
sober and drunk.

If she's not too busy, ask her how
long she's been doing this and how
she has landed her first job.

Step Four

○ When you get home, write down some notes from what you observed.

○ What were the drinks that people ordered?

○ Study your TOP 15 flash cards. Try watching TV, listening to music, or doing household chores as you study. Activity will put your memorization to the test, and the more distractions you can simulate now, the better.

Popular Drinks

....
....
....
....
....
....
....
....
....
....
....

A Bartender's TIP

Bar stools are valuable real-estate. As long as you're drinking, the bartender is happy. But if you switch to water or sit with a glass of ice, don't be surprised to be given a check.

Day 3

Step One

○ Review your flash cards. Set aside the cards you have already successfully memorized.

○ Grab **This Girl Walks Into A Bar** and a highlighter, and mark the recipes in the 100 Drinks section that you saw the bartender make last night.

Step Two

○ Jump back into the kitchen and make those TOP 15 drinks again. Repeat Step 2 from the previous day.

Step Three

○ Create your new resumé. Refer to our suggestions in Chapter Four for guidance. Remember to use nice paper, black ink, and to leave photos of yourself off of it (we've seen it too many times)!

○ Make a list of places in town where you'd love to work. Also check the newspaper and online classifieds like Craigslist to search the "Help Wanted" sections for bartenders.

○ Plan your route to deliver resumés. Sunday and Monday afternoons (non-holiday) are a great time to apply for restaurant jobs. The rush has usually passed and you're more likely to steal five minutes with the manager or owner.

○ Lay out your interview clothes. Keep in mind that you are selling your professionalism and ability to be responsible. So look professional and responsible.

Step Four

○ Step back into the kitchen and cut the rest of the limes and lemons into wedges and twists

○ Make a few more "drinks" from the TOP 15. Remember that you can continue using water and random beverages from the fridge as you get comfortable with the pouring, shaking, mixing, and stirring. Apply whatever techniques you learned from observing the bartender last night.

Step Five

○ Drop off your resumé between 2pm and 5pm. Ask to speak with a manager because there's a strong chance she'll interview you on the spot.

○ Here are a few questions that might come up during an interview:

What they might ask:

Where did you work before?

Can you handle making a lot of drinks at once?

Are you available weekends and holidays?

Can you work the morning or evening shift?

Are you comfortable with a special cocktail menu that changes nightly?

What you might ask:

Do your bartenders free pour or use a jigger?

How many other bartenders will I be working with on my shifts?

Does the staff pool tips?

How do you feel about your bartenders creating original drinks?

○ Write down the manager's name, or the name of the person who took your resumé. Note the date and time that you spoke.

○ If they are hiring, we suspect that you'll be employed on the spot. If there aren't any openings, plan to follow up again in a week if you haven't already landed a gig somewhere else.

Step Six

○ When you get home, make some notes about who you spoke with and what your impressions were of the bar.

○ Plan out which bars to visit with a resumé the next time.

○ Study your flash cards again, then test yourself to see if you can write down the recipe for each drink correctly.

Step Seven

○ If you do have the proper ingredients for any of the TOP 15, now is the time to make a real drink or two. Congratulations! Your 3-Day cram is complete. Toast yourself or invite a friend over to help celebrate your hard work and shiny new skills. You have succeeded in preparing for a wonderful new job!

Notes

13

CHAPTER THIRTEEN
COCKTAIL PARTY 101

Transforming into an exceptional bartender can happen easily and quickly in the comforts of your own home. And in our opinion, mixing a good drink is up there with changing a tire or installing a new belt on your vacuum cleaner. It's just something that a gal should know how to do.

We've outlined the planning part for three different parties:

1 *Intro to Mixers*

2 *Intermediate Soirée*

3 *Advanced Shindig*

You won't need a fancy home bar or an impressive liquor cabinet to get started. All that's required is a patch of counter space, a few basic tools, and a reason to have a party. To really look like a pro refer to Chapter 12 for specific bartending strategies and tips.

Intro to Mixers

The Goal:
To master the Margarita with such authenticity that your guests start speaking Spanish.

The Drink:
Margarita

The Invitees:
5 – 8 People

The Shopping List

Drinks & Accessories:

- 1 bottle of tequila
- 1 bottle of triple sec, Cointreau, or orange liqueur
- 1 large bottle of sweet and sour
- 1 bottle of Rose's lime juice or 10 ounces fresh lime juice
- 10 limes
- 5 lemons
- 1 large bag of ice
- Salt or store bought container of margarita salt
- Lowball glasses or clear plastic cups
- Martini shaker (optional)
- 1 bag of pour spouts
- Cloth or paper napkins

The Preparation:

○ Assuming that each guest (including you) will have two to three Margaritas, cut three limes for a total of 18 wedges and set aside (see page 96).

○ Using Rose's lime juice is easy and convenient. But the difference in taste between the store-bought lime juice and fresh lime juice is dramatic. If you have the time, use a juicer or hand-squeeze the limes into a measuring pitcher to produce about 10 ounces of lime juice. Doing this ahead of time will enable you to produce the drinks quickly once your guests arrive. Cover the pitcher and refrigerate until use.

○ Juice or squeeze the lemons into a small pitcher and refrigerate until use.

○ Pour the sea salt onto a small plate and smooth flat.

Once Your Guests Arrive:

○ Flip to the Margarita recipe.

○ Line up your glasses and pack them with ice.

○ Pour a 2 count (one one-thousand, two one-thousand) of tequila into each glass. The glass may look half full with tequila because of the ice. Pour in one count of triple sec (too much will wreck the drink, so be careful).

○ Pour in sweet and sour just short of the rim, leaving room for the lemon and lime juice.

○ Pour a quick splash of fresh lime juice and lemon juice.

○ For the best tasting Margarita, transfer each drink into a shaker one at a time, then shake or mix.

○ While the ingredients are in the shaker, run a lime along the rim of the glass to make it moist, and set the rim of the glass into the salt.

○ Return the Margarita to a salted glass.

○ Repeat the shaking and salting process for each glass (You can make each drink with the salt on the rim and omit the shaking. However, this often causes a lot of the salt to fall into the drink).

○ Garnish each drink with a lime and serve!

Intermediate Soirée

The Goal:
To serve up three different drinks, make several at once, and maintain poise, charm, and sobriety.

The Drinks:
Cosmopolitan
Manhattan
Salty Dog

The Invitees:
10 – 15 People

The Shopping List

Drinks & Accessories:

1 bottle of vodka

1 bottle of bourbon or whiskey

1 bottle of triple sec or Cointreau

1 small bottle of sweet vermouth

1 small bottle of bitters

1 bottle of Rose's lime juice or fresh lime juice

1 carton of cranberry juice

1 carton of grapefruit juice

1 medium jar of Maraschino cherries

10 limes (5 if you are using Rose's)

Sea salt

1 package of straws (optional)

1 bag of pour spouts

4 bags of ice

Martini and highball glasses, or clear plastic cups

Cloth or paper napkins

Snacks:

Assorted cheeses

Crackers and fruit to pair with the cheeses

Bruschetta

Hot finger foods such as:
mini crab cakes
breaded mushrooms
puffed spinach pastries

Mixed Nuts

Olives

The Preparation:

○ Refrigerate or freeze the liquor until it's time to use.

○ Slice up four of the limes for 24 garnishes (see cutting lemons and limes on page 96).

○ Squeeze or juice the remaining limes and set aside for the Cosmos.

○ Pour the sea salt onto a small plate and smooth flat.

○ If you're using clear plastic cups instead of glass highballs for the Salty Dogs, precut the straws down to a manageable size.

○ Set your bar up next to the sink. If you only have one shaker you'll need to rinse it out well as you switch between the Cosmo and Manhattan. If you have two shakers be sure to dump the ice, but rinsing isn't necessary, as long as you don't mix them up.

○ Neatly arrange the glassware or plastic cups on your counter. Consider setting them on a tray or clean dishtowel.

○ Set out the napkins, cheese, crackers, fruit, and nuts.

- Set out a trash can and a recycling bin.

- Read the cooking instructions for each hot appetizer you'll serve and make a heating schedule for the evening. Plan to bake the appetizer that calls for the most oven time first so that it is ready for your guests when they arrive.

Once Your Guests Arrive:

- Flip to the recipes for the Cosmo, Manhattan, and Salty Dog, and use a sticky note or paper clip to ear mark the pages.

Cosmos and Manhattans:

- Fill a few martini glasses with ice and water to chill.

- Follow our recipe directions for each drink.

- Dump the ice and water out of the martini glass.

- Strain the drink into the glass so that it stops just below the rim.

- You should see some small, thin ice crystals floating on top.

- Garnish with a…

    Cosmo: Lime

    Manhattan: Cherry

    Salty Dogs: Moisten the rim of the glass with a lime, then dip the rim into the salt.

A Bartender's **TIP**

Want to know the secret to carrying full martini glasses across a crowded room? Don't look at the glass as you walk! Imagine you are holding a pencil or the stem of a flower as you approach your guest, and not a single drop will escape that little glass.

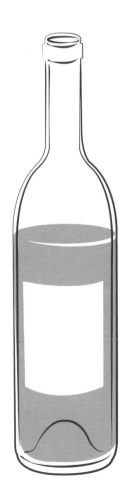

Advanced Shindig

The Goal:

To pump out drink after drink while sustaining conversations, avoiding excessive perspiration, and flirting with your cute neighbor.

The Drinks:

Choose 6 from our list of 100, or prepare the following:

Martini
Long Island Iced Tea
Lemon Drop
Cadillac
Margarita
MaiTai
Whiskey Sour

The Invitees:

20 – 25 People (or more!)

A Bartender's TIP

The following shopping list will provide for drinks beyond the "featured" ones listed above. You'll be able to honor requests for Cuba Libres, Screwdrivers, Vodka Tonics, Tom Collins, and more.

The Shopping List

Drinks & Accessories:

1 bottle of vodka
1 bottle of bourbon or whiskey
1 bottle of light rum
1 bottle of dark rum
1 bottle of tequila
1 bottle of gin
3 large bottles of sweet n' sour mix
1 small bottle of triple sec or Cointreau
1 bottle of Rose's lime juice or fresh lime juice
1 small bottle of grenadine
2 liters of club soda
2 liters of tonic water
2 liters of Coke
1 liter of Diet Coke
1 liter of 7Up
1 carton of orange juice
1 carton of cranberry juice
1 carton of lemonade
2 bottles of sweet & sour
20 limes
(10 if you are using Rose's lime juice)
10 lemons
1 orange
1 large jar of olives
1 medium jar of Maraschino cherries
Salt
Sugar
Cloth napkins or 1 package of heavy weight paper napkins
Highball, lowball, and martini glasses or 2 packages (50 – 100) of clear plastic cups
1 small box of toothpicks
8 large bags of ice
Martini shaker
Plastic tubs to store the ice

The Preparation

o Refrigerate or freeze the liquor until use.

o Clean the plastic tubs you will use to store your ice. If you decide to store your ice bags in the bathtub, be sure to line your tub with trash bags.

o Slice half of the lemons and limes for drink garnishes. Store them in separate containers to prevent the fruits from sharing flavors, and refrigerate.

o For the other half of the lemons and limes, use a juicer or hand-squeeze them into a measuring pitcher to use for the drink recipes. Doing this ahead of time will enable you to produce the drinks quickly once your guests arrive. Cover the pitchers and refrigerate until use.

o Prepare lemon twists (see page 96).

o Pour the sea salt onto a small plate and smooth flat.

o Pour the sugar onto a small plate and smooth flat.

o Set up your bar next to the sink.

o Spread out a few dish towels on the counter to absorb splashes, spills, and overflows.

o If you only have one sink, keep it clear for rinsing out your shaker and dumping empty cocktails. If you have two sinks, use the second one for storing ice. Place a large bowl inside the sink for the ice or line the sink with a trash bag.

o Arrange your liquor bottles on the counter along the wall and make sure each one has a pour spout.

o Put the bowls of lemon wedges and lime wedges within reach. Don't mix them together because they will share flavors.

o Set out a trash can and a recycling bin.

o Read the cooking instructions for each hot appetizer you'll serve and make a heating schedule for the evening. Plan to bake the appetizer that calls for the most oven time first so that it is ready for your guests when they arrive.

A Bartender's TIP

Need a conspicuous cheat sheet? Copy some of the recipes onto sticky notes and place them inside the refrigerator, cupboards, and drawers.

Once Your Guests Arrive

o Serve your friends as they arrive, but once the party gets busy, take drink orders in groups. This way you can get the practice you need by making two or three drinks at a time.

o Some people may offer to make their own cocktail when they see how hard you are working. Thank them and reassure them that you're having fun!

o During the first part of the evening you might not leave the bar area, but once things get going, you'll have time to socialize, and enjoy one of your own perfect cocktails.

Extra Party Prep Tidbits

○ If you're using real glassware, make sure it's spot and chip free.

○ Put a rug under your bar area to catch the spills. They're guaranteed to happen, even before the intoxication sets in and table dancing begins.

○ Put two trash cans near the bar: one for garbage and one for recyclables.

○ If you're using real wine and martini glasses, drink charms are a must! Otherwise you'll be washing dishes all night long.

○ Background music is great, especially in the beginning when that first eager beaver shows up. Keep it low and make adjustments as the night goes on.

Cocktail Party 101

If your gathering requires more than just beer and wine, this list will help you select a well-matched drink for your event.

New Year's Eve

New Year's Day

Super Bowl Sunday

Valentine's Day

Oscar Night

St. Patrick's Day

Easter

Cinco de Mayo

July 4th

Labor Day

Halloween

Thanksgiving

Christmas

Bachelorette Party

Baby Shower

14

CHAPTER FOURTEEN
HOME MIXOLOGY

Back in the day, men made the martinis and women made the meatloaf. Now we do both. But we're taking it a step further than simply constructing the old cocktail favorites with perfection. Women are joining bars and restaurants in the global trend of creating original drinks from both everyday and unusual ingredients.

Conjuring up a drink isn't as hard as you may think. Remember when you were a kid in the kitchen, following imaginary recipes that involved any ingredient from the fridge or pantry that you could get your hands on? Building a new cocktail will bring back that same inspired artistry only this time you'll want someone other than your mom to taste it.

Liquor

To get started as a mixologist, you don't need much. If you have a few spirits, liqueurs, and mixers in your home, begin with those. If your liquor cabinet is bare, you have two options:

Build-a-Bar Option #1

Whenever you visit the market, depending on how frequently you go, pick up a new spirit or liqueur. Build your alcohol collection at your own pace. Avoid buying any mixers that don't require refrigeration once opened. They're usually loaded with high fructose corn syrup and few fresh ingredients.

Build-a-Bar Option #2

For those of you who are in a hurry to get your home bar up and running, purchase what you need for a Long Island and Long Beach Iced Tea. They share all of the same ingredients except for one: a Long Island takes Coke and a Long Beach calls for cranberry juice. The rest of your shopping list will include tequila, vodka, gin, rum, triple sec, and sweet & sour. Imagine all the drinks you can make from those eight ingredients!

Ingredients

When it comes to the ingredients of your drinks, be as conservative or daring as you desire. Making a cocktail that tastes good enough to serve to others should be your first priority. Your second priority is the presentation. Elaborate garnishes, custom shaped ice cubes, and jaw-dropping ingredients are all fine as long as the drink won't fall over, explode, or crawl once served.

Here's a list of some ingredients we've used in our own drinks or tasted in someone else's. Mix, match, fill in the blanks, or add more categories of your own — just have fun. Creating an original cocktail is all about trial and error.

CITRUS	FRUITS	VEGGIES	TEAS	SWEETS	SIMPLE SYRUPS	SPICES / HERBS
Clementine	Apple	Beet	Black	Brown Sugar	Ginger Syrup	Apple Pie Spice
Grapefruit	Apricot	Bell Pepper	Chai	Chocolate	Lemon Syrup	Basil
Orange	Banana	Celery	Chamomile	Chocolate Bar	Mint Syrup	Chili Powder
Lemon	Blackberry	Dandelion	Cinnamon	Chocolate Drops	Sugar Syrup	Cinnamon
Lime	Blueberry	Endive	Darjeeling	Donuts		Cinnamon Sticks
Tangerine	Cantaloupe	Fiddlehead	Earl Grey	Girl Scout Cookies		Lemon Grass
	Cranberry	Pumpkin	English Breakfast	Gum Drops		Nutmeg
	Cherry	Radish	Ginseng	Gummy Bears		Paprika
	Fig	Sweet Pepper	Green	Gummy Worms		Pepper
	Grape	Watercress	Japanese	Ice Cream		Pumpkin Spice
	Guavaberry		Jasmine	Jelly Beans		Rosemary
	Kumquat		Mint	Jelly Belly		
	Kiwi		Peppermint	Lemon Drops		
	Mango			Licorice		
	Papaya			Lolly Pops		
	Pear			Marshmallow		
	Peach			Nutella		
	Pineapple			Peanut Butter Cups		
	Plum			Peppermint Sticks		
	Raspberry			Powered Sugar		
	Strawberry			Sprinkles		
	Watermelon					

HOME MIXOLOGY TOOLS

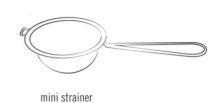

mini strainer

blender

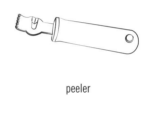

peeler

measuring spoons

melon baller

juicer

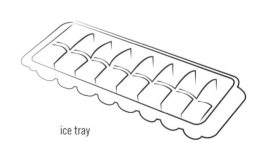

ice tray

ice cream scoop

garlic press

1 oz
½ oz

jigger

citrus squeezer

wine / beer opener

straws

toothpicks

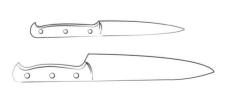

knives

cutting board

PROFESSIONAL BARWARE

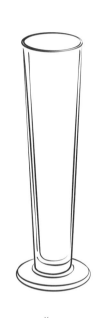

pilsner

red wine

white wine

sherry / port

1 oz

½ oz

jigger

coffee

champagne flute

shot

lowball

shaker

brandy snifter

rocks

cork screw

margarita

bar spoon

pint glass

martini

highball

strainer

CUTTING LIME OR LEMON GARNISHES

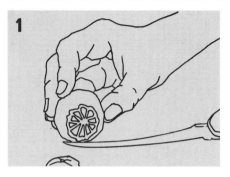

1

To make wedges, cut off the ends of the lemon or lime so that the fruit can stand upright with the original oval shape still intact.

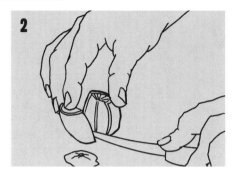

2

Cut the lime or lemon in half. Then cut each half into three wedges.

CUTTING LONG LEMON TWISTS

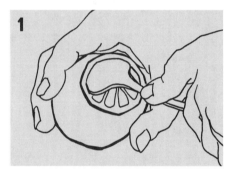

1

Begin with step 1 from above. Carefully slide a spoon between the peel and the flesh and work your way around the inside of the lemon until the two are no longer attached.

2

Push the flesh of the lemon out through one of the ends so that you are left with a hollow lemon peel.

CUTTING SHORT LEMON TWISTS

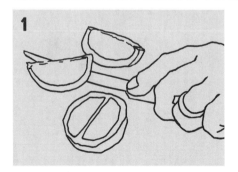

1

Cut the tips off of both ends of the lemon and cut it into quarters.

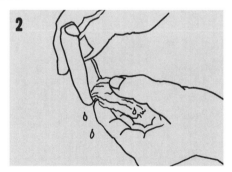

2

Slide the tip of a spoon between the skin of the lemon and the flesh. Using your hands, gently pull the flesh away from the peel until they are separate.

3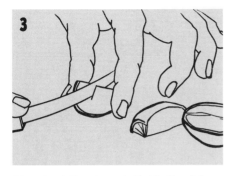

Using a sharp knife, make a vertical incision through the center of each wedge without going through the outside skin.

4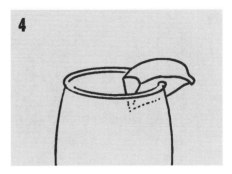

Use the slits as hooks for the rims of glasses.

3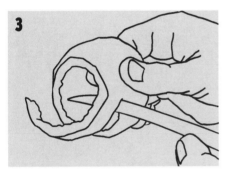

Using a sharp knife, begin cutting the lemon as if you were peeling an apple into one continuous strip.

4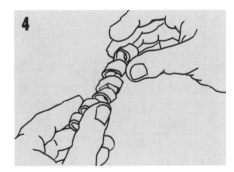

Cut the long curly Q into four pieces and twist each piece to form spirals.

3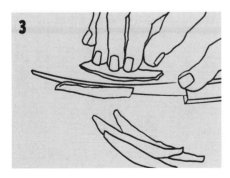

Slice the peel length-wise into strips the width of an eyeliner pencil.

4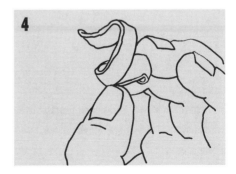

Twist the strips until they make a curly Q.

Acknowledgments

Jordan

The insight, inspiration and support for this book came from our amazing family and friends. For your repeated reads and long friendships, thanks to Alyssa, Jen, Lauren, and Marta. Thanks to Carol Kushner for her editing assistance, Lauren Franca for her photography talents, and to Bianca Rehm for her gracious hosting. To the fantastic bar bosses who made going to work easy, thanks to Cindy Meadows, Sig Ortloff, and Captain Ron Schur. Big thank you to all the regulars I've had the opportunity to know, especially at The Galley, who grew from customers to friends. Thank you to our parents for instilling from an early age the belief that any dream is possible. Thanks Dad, for your superior editing and writing skills and Mom, for your gifted artistry. Thank you to my husband, whose endless support, encouragement and love drives my motivation. And thank you to my dear sister for your talent, creativity, tireless enthusiasm, and life-long friendship.

Jocelyn

Thank you to my parents for encouraging me to pursue a creative career. Thanks to Gale Okumura, GFDG, Knock Knock, Sargent & Berman, and Department of Graphic Sciences for contributing to my growth as a graphic designer. Thanks to Marta, Carrie, Sara, Ashley, Lindsay, and Kavita for your read-throughs and comments, and especially to Cara for your many design "crits" and valuable feedback. Thank you to my incredible husband, who inspires me to work hard and supports my non-traditional career path. And thanks to my extraordinary big sis, whose drive and unstoppable entrepreneurial spirit motivates me daily.

Editing: Ingrid de Haas and Ross E. Dunn
Personal Story and "girl head" illustrations: Tom Tierney
Demonstration drawings, pages 96 – 97: Jeanne Dunn
Photography: Lauren Franca

ABOUT US

Jordan Catapano

Jordan has had long experience as a professional bartender and mixologist. In 2010 she and her sister co-founded their lifestyle and entertaining business, This Girl Walks Into a Bar. She blogs daily for their website and regularly writes for Beverages & More and Modern Mom. Jordan's drink recipes and cocktail photography have been featured in Women's Day Magazine, Saveur.com, PBS.com, and Glo.com. Her mixology has also been commissioned by companies like Dole Foods, Caesarstone, Thermador, California Black Olive, and Bungalow Clothing. She lives in Los Angeles with her husband and children.

Jocelyn Dunn Muhlbach

Jocelyn Dunn Muhlbach, the graphic designer behind This Girl Walks Into A Bar, created and maintains the company's brand image and produces all artwork for their website, books, and product line. Her background includes work for a wide array of clientele, including Disney, University of California Los Angeles, Westfield, Princess Cruises, Anne Taintor, E!, Knock Knock, Sony Pictures, Pottery Barn, Dreamworks, and Mattel. She lives in Los Angeles with her husband and daughter.

100
COCKTAIL
RECIPE
FLASH CARDS

Amaretto Sour

Alabama Slammer
(shot)

Apple Martini

B52
(shot)

AMARETTO SOUR

Jigger

Fill glass with ice
2 ounces amaretto
2 ounces sweet n' sour
Stir to mix
Garnish with a cherry

Free Pour

Fill glass with ice
2 counts amaretto
Fill the rest of glass with sweet n' sour
Stir to mix
Garnish with a cherry

ALABAMA SLAMMER (SHOT)

Jigger

Fill shaker with ice
1/2 ounce amaretto
1/2 ounce sloe gin
1/2 ounce Southern Comfort
Splash of sweet n' sour
Squeeze of lemon juice
Shake together and strain into
a shot glass

Free Pour

Fill shaker with ice
1 count amaretto
1 count sloe gin
1 count Southern Comfort
Splash of sweet n' sour
Squeeze of lemon juice
Shake together and strain into a shot glass

APPLE MARTINI

Jigger

Fill shaker with ice
2 ounces vodka
1 ounce apple liquor
Splash sweet n' sour
Shake and strain into glass
Garnish with cherry

Free Pour

Fill shaker with ice
4 counts vodka
2 counts apple liquor
Splash sweet n' sour
Shake and strain into glass
Garnish with cherry

B52 (SHOT)

Jigger

Fill shaker with ice
1/2 ounce coffee liqueur
1/2 ounce Irish cream liqueur
1/2 ounce Cointreau or triple sec
Shake once and strain into
a shot glass

Free Pour

Fill shaker with ice
1 count coffee liqueur
1 count Irish cream liqueur
1 count Cointreau or triple sec
Shake once and strain into shot glass

Bay Breeze

Bellini

Black and Tan

Black Russian

BAY BREEZE

Jigger

Fill shaker with ice
2 ounces vodka
1 ounce cranberry juice
1 ounce pineapple juice
Stir to mix then serve

Free Pour

Fill shaker with ice
2 counts vodka
1 count cranberry juice
1 count pineapple juice
Stir to mix then serve

BELLINI

Jigger

1 ounce peach schnapps
4-5 ounces champagne
When filling glass, hold
champagne glass at a slight
angle to avoid an overflow

Free Pour

Splash of peach schnapps
Fill glass with champagne

BLACK AND TAN

Jigger

Can of pale ale
Can of Guiness Stout Beer
Pour pale ale into a 16 ounce glass. Using the back of a spoon,
slowly add the Guinness to the pale ale to create the layered,
or "black and tan" effect.

BLACK RUSSIAN

Jigger

Fill glass with ice
1 1/2 ounces vodka
1 measure coffee liqueur
Stir to mix then serve

Free Pour

Fill glass with ice
2 counts vodka
1 count coffee liqueur
Stir to mix then serve

Bloody Maria

Bloody Mary

Bloody Mary Mix
(serves 4-6)

Blue Hawaiian

BLOODY MARIA

Jigger

Fill glass with ice
2 ounces tequila
3 ounces Bloody Mary mix
1 teaspoon lemon juice
1 teaspoon lime juice
Shake well
Garnish with 2 olives and a lime
Salted rim optional

Free Pour

Fill glass with ice
2 counts tequila
3 counts Bloody Mary mix
Squeeze of lemon wedge
Squeeze of lime wedge
Shake well
Garnish with 2 olives and a lime
Salted rim optional

BLOODY MARY

Jigger

Fill glass with ice
2 ounces vodka
3 ounces Bloody Mary mix
1 teaspoon lemon juice
1 teaspoon lime juice
Shake well
Garnish with 2 olives and a lime
Salted rim optional

Free Pour

Fill glass with ice
2 ounces vodka
3 counts Bloody Mary mix
Squeeze of lemon wedge
Squeeze of lime wedge
Shake well
Garnish with 2 olives and a lime
Salted rim optional

BLOODY MARY MIX (SERVES 4-6)

Jigger

1 large can tomato juice
2 ounces of horse radish
2 ounces Worcestershire sauce
1/2 ounce Tobasco sauce
1/2 lemon
1/2 lime
1 tablespoon pepper
1 teaspoon salt

BLUE HAWAIIAN

Jigger

Fill bucket glass with ice
1 ounce light rum
1 ounce Blue Curacao
1 ounce cream of coconut
2 ounces pineapple juice
Stir or shake once and garnish
with a cherry

Free Pour

Fill bucket glass with ice
2 counts light rum
2 counts Blue Curacao
2 counts cream of coconut
Fill the rest of the glass with pineapple juice
Garnish with a cherry

Brave Bull

Buttery Nipple
(shot)

Cape Cod

Casablanca

BRAVE BULL

Jigger

Fill rocks glass with ice
2 ounces tequila
1 ounce coffee liqueur
Stir to mix then serve

Free Pour

Fill rocks glass with ice
2 counts tequila
1 count coffee liqueur
Stir to mix then serve

BUTTERY NIPPLE (SHOT)

Jigger

Fill shaker with ice
1 ounce vodka
1 ounce Irish cream liqueur
1 ounce butterscotch schnapps
Shake and strain into a shot glass

Free Pour

Fill shaker with ice
1 count vodka
1 ounce Irish cream liqueur
1 ounce butterscotch schnapps
Shake and strain into a shot glass

CAPE COD

Jigger

Fill glass with ice
2 ounces vodka
3 ounces cranberry juice
Stir to mix
Garnish with a lime

Free Pour

Fill glass with ice
2 counts vodka
2 counts cranberry juice
Stir to mix
Garnish with a lime

CASABLANCA

Jigger

Fill glass with ice
1 ounce light rum
1 ounce Malibu rum
1 ounce triple sec
1 ounce pineapple juice
Splash grenadine
Stir to mix and garnish
with slice of pineapple or cherry

Free Pour

Fill glass with ice
1 count light rum
1 count Malibu rum
1 count triple sec
Fill the rest of the glass with pineapple
Splash grenadine
Stir to mix and garnish with slice
of pineapple or cherry

Champagne Cocktail

Chocolate Martini

Cosmopolitan

Cuba Libre

CHAMPAGNE COCKTAIL

Jigger

1 sugar cube
1-2 dashes of Angostura bitters
6 ounces champagne
When filling glass, hold champagne glass
at a slight angle to avoid an overflow

CHOCOLATE MARTINI

Jigger

Fill shaker with ice
2 ounces vodka
1 ounce chocolate liqueur
1 ounce half & half

Free Pour

Fill shaker with ice
2 counts vodka
1 count chocolate liqueur
Splash of half & half

Shake hard until frothy. Drizzle chocolate around inside of martini glass,
then strain ingredients into glass

COSMOPOLITAN

Jigger

Fill shaker with ice
3 ounces vodka
1/2 ounce triple sec
Splash of cranberry juice
Squeeze of lime
Shake hard and strain in glass
Garnish with a lime

Free Pour

Fill shaker with ice
4 counts vodka
Splash triple sec
Splash of cranberry juice
Squeeze of lime
Shake hard and strain in glass
Garnish with a lime

CUBA LIBRE

Jigger

Fill bucket glass with ice
2 ounces rum
2 ounces Coke
Garnish with a lime

Free Pour

Fill bucket glass with ice
2 counts rum
Fill rest of glass with Coke
Garnish with a lime

Dirty Martini

Dreamsicle

Eggnog Rum

French Connection

DIRTY MARTINI

Jigger

Fill shaker with ice
3 ounces vodka
Drip of vermouth
1/2 - 1 ounce olive juice
Shake hard and strain into glass
Garnish with olives

Free Pour

Fill shaker with ice
4 counts vodka
Drip of vermouth
Splash of olive juice
Shake hard and strain into glass
Garnish with olives

DREAMSICLE

Jigger

Fill shaker with ice
2 ounces vanilla vodka
1 ounce pineapple juice
1 ounce cream
Splash gingerale
Shake until frothy
Strain into chilled glass

Free Pour

Fill shaker with ice
2 counts vodka
1 count pineapple juice
1 count cream
Splash gingerale
Shake until frothy
Strain into chilled glass

EGGNOG RUM

Jigger

Fill shaker with ice
2 ounces light rum
1 ounce amaretto
2 ounces eggnog
Shake until frothy and strain
into glass
Dust the top with sprinkling
of cinnamon

Free Pour

Fill shaker with ice
2 counts light rum
1 count amaretto
2 counts eggnog
Shake until frothy and strain
into glass
Dust the top with sprinkling
of cinnamon

FRENCH CONNECTION

Jigger

Fill glass with ice
2 ounces brandy
1 ounce amaretto
Stir to mix then serve

Free Pour

Fill glass with ice
2 counts brandy
1 count amaretto
Stir to mix then serve

Fuzzy Navel

Gibson

Gimlet

Godfather

FUZZY NAVEL

Jigger

Fill glass with ice
2 ounces peach schnapps
4 ounces orange juice
Stir and garnish with an orange

Free Pour

Fill glass with ice
2 counts peach schnapps
Fill the rest of the glass with orange juice
Stir and garnish with an orange

GIBSON

Jigger

Fill shaker with ice
3 ounces gin
Drip of vermouth
Shake hard and strain into glass
Garnish with onion

Free Pour

Fill shaker with ice
4 counts vodka
Drip of vermouth
Shake hard and strain into glass
Garnish with onion

GIMLET

Jigger

Fill shaker with ice
3 ounces vodka
1 teaspoon Rose's lime juice
Squeeze of fresh lime juice
Shake hard and strain into glass
Garnish with wedge of lime

Free Pour

Fill shaker with ice
4 counts vodka
Splash of Rose's lime juice
Squeeze of fresh lime juice
Shake hard and strain into glass
Garnish with wedge of lime

GODFATHER

Jigger

Fill glass with ice
2 ounces scotch
1 ounce amaretto
Stir to mix then serve

Free Pour

Fill glass with ice
2 counts scotch
1 count amaretto
Stir to mix then serve

Grasshopper

Grey Hound

Harvey Wallbanger

Hawaiian Punch

GRASSHOPPER

Jigger

Fill glass with ice
1 1/2 ounces crème de cacao
1 1/2 ounces crème de menthe
Splash of milk or cream

Free Pour

Fill glass with ice
2 counts crème de cacao
2 counts crème de menthe
Splash of milk or cream

Pour ice and ingredients into a shaker to mix around,
then pour back into glass and serve.

GREY HOUND

Jigger

Fill glass with ice
2 ounces vodka
3 ounces grapefruit juice
Stir to mix then serve

Free Pour

Fill glass with ice
2 counts vodka
3 counts grapefruit juice
Stir to mix then serve

HARVEY WALLBANGER

Jigger

Fill glass with ice
2 ounces vodka
2 ounces orange juice
Splash of Galliano floater on top
Garnish with an orange twist

Free Pour

Fill glass with ice
2 counts vodka
Pour in orange juice almost to the top
Pour in a floater of Galliano to the top
Garnish with an orange twist

HAWAIIAN PUNCH

Jigger

Fill glass with ice
1/2 ounce rum, 1/2 ounce vodka
1/2 ounce amaretto
1/2 ounce raspberry liqueur
1 ounce orange juice
1 ounce pineapple juice
Splash of grenadine syrup

Free Pour

Fill glass with ice
1 count rum, 1 count vodka
1 count amaretto
Splash of raspberry liqueur & grenadine syrup
Fill the rest of the glass up with orange juice
and pineapple juice

Mix in shaker with ice, pour into a glass and garnish with cherry & pineapple slice

Hot Toddy

Irish Car Bomb

Irish Coffee

Italian Coffee

HOT TODDY

Jigger

2 ounces bourbon or whiskey
1 teaspoon of powdered sugar
1/2 teaspoon lemon juice
1/8 teaspoon cinnamon
1 clove
4 ounces boiling water
Garnish with a cinnamon stick

Free Pour

2 counts bourbon or whiskey
Small spoon of powdered sugar
Squeeze of a lemon wedge
Dash of cinnamon
1 clove
Fill coffee mug or tea cup with hot water
Garnish with a cinnamon stick

IRISH CAR BOMB

Jigger

1/2 ounce Irish cream
1/2 Irish whiskey
Mix ingredients and set aside
Fill a pint glass 3/4 full with Guinness
Drop the shot glass into the beer
and serve immediately

Free Pour

Fill a shot glass with Irish cream
and Irish whiskey
Fill a pint glass 3/4 full with a Guinness
Drop the shot glass into the beer
and serve immediately

IRISH COFFEE

Jigger

2 ounces Irish whiskey
4 ounces coffee
Garnish with whipped cream

Free Pour

2 counts Irish whiskey
Fill mug with coffee
Garnish with whipped cream

ITALIAN COFFEE

Jigger

1 ounce brandy
1 ounce amaretto
4 ounces coffee
Garnish with whipped cream

Free Pour

1 count brandy
1 count amaretto
Fill the coffee cup with coffee
Garnish with whipped cream

Jack & Double Ginger

Jell-O Shot

John Collins

Junior

JACK & DOUBLE GINGER

Jigger

Fill glass with ice
2 ounces Jack Daniels
2 ounces gingerale
1 ounce fresh ginger juice
Garnish with lemon twist

Free Pour

Fill glass with ice
2 counts Jack Daniels
A spoonful of ginger juice
Fill the rest of the glass with gingerale
Garnish with lemon twist

JELL-O SHOT

Jigger

1 package of Jell-O gelatin (choose your flavor)
6 ounces of boiling water
6 ounces of vodka or light rum*
*Get creative with your liquor choices!
Mix all the ingredients together and pour into shot glasses, an ice cube tray,
or little paper cups
Refrigerate until Jell-O is cool and firm
Serve in the cups or pop the cubes out from the ice cube tray and serve in a bowl

JOHN COLLINS

Jigger

Fill glass with ice
2 ounces whiskey or bourbon
1/2 packet sugar
1/2 ounce soda water
1/2 ounce Sprite or 7Up
1 ounce sweet n' sour
Squeeze of lemon wedge
Garnish with lemon wedge

Free Pour

Fill glass with ice
2 counts whiskey or bourbon
1/2 packet sugar
Splash soda water
Splash Sprite or 7Up
Fill the rest of the glass with sweet n' sour
Squeeze of lemon wedge
Garnish with lemon wedge

JUNIOR

Jigger

Fill shaker with ice
3 ounces peach vodka
1/2 ounce lemon juice
1/2 ounce lime juice
1/2 ounce orange juice
1/2 ounce of cranberry juice
Shake hard and strain into glass
Garnish with a peach slice

Free Pour

Fill shaker with ice
4 counts of peach vodka
Squeeze of lemon
Squeeze of lime
Squeeze of orange
Splash of cranberry juice
Shake hard and strain into glass
Garnish with a peach slice

Kamikaze

Keoke Coffee

Key Lime Martini

Kicktail

KAMIKAZE

Jigger

Fill shaker with ice
1 1/2 ounces vodka
1/2 ounce triple sec
1/2 ounce of lime juice
Shake and strain into glass
Garnish with lime

Free Pour

Fill shaker with ice
3 counts vodka
Splash triple sec
2 squeezes of lime
Shake and strain into glass
Garnish with lime

KEOKE COFFEE

Jigger

1/2 ounce Kahlua
1/2 ounce brandy
1/2 ounce crème de cocao
3 ounces coffee
Garnish with whipped cream

Free Pour

Splash Kahlua
Splash brandy
Splash crème de cocao
Fill the rest of the mug with coffee
Garnish with whipped cream

KEY LIME MARTINI

Jigger

Fill shaker with ice
2 ounces vanilla vodka
1 ounce pineapple juice
1 ounce Rose's lime juice
Squeeze of lime wedge
1/2 ounce half & half
Shake and strain into glass

Free Pour

Fill shaker with ice
3 counts vanilla vodka
Splash pineapple juice
Splash Rose's lime juice
Squeeze of lime wedge
Splash half & half
Shake and strain into glass

KICKTAIL

Jigger

Fill shaker with ice
2 ounces pepper vodka
1 ounce lemon liqueur
1/2 teaspoon wasabi
Shake and strain into glass
Garnish with lemon twist

Free Pour

Fill shaker with ice
4 counts pepper vodka
Splash lemon liqueur
Small drop of wasabi
Shake and strain into glass
Garnish with lemon twist

Kir

Kir Royale

Lemon Drop

Long Beach

KIR

Jigger

1 teaspoon crème de cassis
6 ounces of white wine
Garnish with lemon twist

Free Pour

Splash of crème de cassis
Fill the rest of the glass with white wine
Garnish with lemon twist

KIR ROYALE

Jigger

1 teaspoon crème de cassis
6 ounces of champagne
Garnish with lemon twist

Free Pour

Splash of crème de cassis
Fill the rest of the glass with champagne
Garnish with lemon twist

LEMON DROP

Jigger

Fill shaker with ice
2 ounces lemon vodka
1/2 ounce sweet n' sour
1/2 ounce triple sec
1/2 ounce of lemon juice

Free Pour

Fill shaker with ice
4 counts lemon vodka
Splash sweet n' sour
Dash of triple sec
2 squeezes of lemon

Shake and strain into a glass with a sugar coated rim

LONG BEACH

Jigger

Fill glass with ice
1 ounce vodka
1 ounce gin
1 ounce rum
1 ounce tequila
1/2 ounce cranberry juice
1/2 ounce sweet n' sour
Garnish with a lemon wedge

Free Pour

Fill glass with ice
1 count vodka
1 count gin
1 count rum
1 count tequila
Splash cranberry juice
Fill the rest of glass with sweet n' sour
Garnish with a lemon wedge

Long Island

Madras

Mai Tai

Manhattan

LONG ISLAND

Jigger

Fill glass with ice
1 ounce vodka, 1 ounce gin
1 ounce rum, 1 ounce tequila
1/2 ounce triple sec
1/2 ounce Coke
1/2 ounce sweet n' sour
Garnish with a lemon wedge

Free Pour

Fill glass with ice
1 count vodka, 1 count gin
1 count rum, 1 count tequila
Splash triple sec
Splash Coke
Fill the rest of glass with sweet n' sour
Garnish with a lemon wedge

MADRAS

Jigger

Fill glass with ice
2 ounces vodka
2 ounces orange juice
2 ounces cranberry juice
Stir to mix then serve

Free Pour

Fill glass with ice
2 counts vodka
1 count orange juice
1 count cranberry juice
Stir to mix then serve

MAI TAI

Jigger

Fill glass with ice
2 ounces light rum
1/2 ounce pineapple juice
1/2 ounce orange juice
1/2 ounce sweet n' sour
1/2 ounce grenadine
1 ounce dark rum floater
Garnish with a lime and cherry

Free Pour

Fill glass with ice
2 counts light rum
Splash pineapple juice
Splash orange juice
Splash sweet n' sour
Splash grenadine
1 count dark rum floater
Garnish with a lime and cherry

MANHATTAN

Jigger

Fill shaker with ice
3 ounces whiskey
1 teaspoon sweet vermouth
1/8 teaspoon of bitters
Shake and strain into glass
Garnish with a cherry

Free Pour

Fill shaker with ice
3 counts whiskey
Splash sweet vermouth
2 squirts of bitters
Shake and strain into glass
Garnish with a cherry

Margarita

Margarita, Cadillac

Martini

Melon Ball

MARGARITA

Jigger

Fill glass with ice
2 ounces tequila
1/2 ounce of triple sec
2 ounces sweet n' sour
Squeeze of two lime wedges
Squeeze of two lemon wedges
Stir and garnish with a lime

Free Pour

Fill glass with ice
3 counts tequila
Splash of triple sec
2 counts sweet n' sour
Squeeze of two lime wedges
Squeeze of two lemon wedges
Stir and garnish with a lime

MARGARITA, CADILLAC

Jigger

Fill glass with ice
2 ounces tequila
1/2 ounce of triple sec
2 ounces sweet n' sour
Squeeze of two lime wedges
Squeeze of two lemon wedges
Stir or mix in shaker
1/2 - 1 ounce Grand Marnier floater
Stir and garnish with a lime

Free Pour

Fill glass with ice
3 counts tequila
Splash of triple sec
2 counts sweet n' sour
Squeeze of two lime wedges
Squeeze of two lemon wedges
Stir or mix in shaker
1/2 - 1 ounce Grand Marnier floater
Stir and garnish with a lime

MARTINI

Jigger

Fill shaker with ice
3 ounces vodka
Drip of vermouth (optional)
Shake hard and strain into glass
Garnish with olives

Free Pour

Fill shaker with ice
4 counts vodka
Drip of vermouth (optional)
Shake hard and strain into glass
Garnish with olives

MELON BALL

Jigger

Fill glass with ice
2 ounces vodka
1 ounces melon liqueur
2 ounces orange juice
Garnish with melon ball
or orange slice

Free Pour

Fill glass with ice
2 counts vodka
1 count melon liqueur
Fill the rest of the glass with orange juice
Garnish with melon ball or orange slice

Mexican Coffee

Midori Sour

Mimosa

Mind Eraser

MEXICAN COFFEE

Jigger

2 ounces tequila
1 ounce Kahlua
4 ounces coffee

Free Pour

2 counts tequila
1 count Kahlua
Fill mug with coffee

MIDORI SOUR

Jigger

Fill glass with ice
2 ounces Midori liqueur
2 ounces sweet n' sour
Garnish with cherry

Free Pour

Fill glass with ice
2 counts Midori liqueur
Fill the rest of the glass with sweet n' sour
Garnish with cherry

MIMOSA

Jigger

4 ounces champagne
2 ounces orange juice

Free Pour

Fill flute 3/4 with champagne
Fill the rest of the glass with orange juice

MIND ERASER

Jigger

Fill glass with ice
1 ounce vodka
1 ounce coffee liqueur
2 ounces soda water

Free Pour

Fill glass with ice
1 count vodka
1 count coffee liqueur
Fill the rest of the glass with soda water

Mint Julep

Mojito

Moroccan Mojito

Mudslide
(can also be blended)

MINT JULEP

Jigger
Fill glass with ice
2 ounces bourbon
2 ounces mint simple syrup*
Garnish with a mint sprig

Free Pour
Fill glass with ice
2 counts bourbon
Fill the rest of the glass with mint simple syrup*
Garnish with a mint sprig

*Mint Simple Syrup (1 part water to 1 part sugar)
1 package mint leaves, finely chopped, 2-3 tablespoons sugar, 2-3 ounces water

MOJITO

Jigger
Fill glass with ice
2 ounces light rum
2 ounces mint simple syrup*
2 ounces soda water
1/2 ounce lime juice
Garnish with a mint sprig

Free Pour
Fill glass with ice
3 counts light rum
2 counts mint simple syrup
1 count soda water
Squeeze of lime juice
Garnish with a mint sprig

*Mint Simple Syrup (1 part water to 1 part sugar)
1 package mint leaves, finely chopped, 2-3 tablespoons sugar, 2-3 ounces water

MOROCCAN MOJITO

Jigger
Fill glass with ice
2 ounces light rum
2 ounces mint simple syrup*
1 teaspoon ginger juice
2 ounces tonic water

Free Pour
Fill glass with ice
3 counts light rum
2 counts mint simple syrup
1/2 spoonful of ginger juice
Fill the rest of the glass with tonic water

*Mint Simple Syrup (1 part water to 1 part sugar)
1 package mint leaves, finely chopped, 2-3 tablespoons sugar, 2-3 ounces water

MUDSLIDE (CAN ALSO BE BLENDED)

Jigger
Fill glass with ice
1 ounce vodka
1 ounce coffee liqueur
1 ounce Irish cream
1 ounce half & half
1/2 ounce chocolate syrup
Stir or shake ingredients and serve

Free Pour
Fill glass with ice
1 count vodka
1 count coffee liqueur
1 count Irish cream
1 count half & half
Splash chocolate syrup
Stir or shake ingredients and serve

Negroni

Old Fashioned

Orgasm
(Shot)

Pali Blue Breeze

NEGRONI

Jigger

Fill glass with ice
1 ounce gin
1 ounce sweet vermouth
1 ounce Campari
Stir to mix
Garnish with a lemon twist

Free Pour

Fill glass with ice
1 count gin
1 count sweet vermouth
1 count Campari
Stir to mix
Garnish with a lemon twist

OLD FASHIONED

Jigger

Fill glass with ice
2 ounces bourbon
1 teaspoon Angostura bitters
1/2 ounce simple syrup*
Stir to mix
Garnish with cherry and orange twist

Free Pour

Fill glass with ice
2 counts bourbon
3 dashes bitters
Spoonful of simple syrup*
Garnish with cherry and orange twist

*Simple Syrup (1 part water to 1 part sugar)
1/2 ounce = 1 tablespoon, 1 tablespoon water, 1 tablespoon sugar

ORGASM (SHOT)

Jigger

1/2 ounce vodka
1/2 ounce crème de cacao
1/2 ounce amaretto
1/2 ounce triple sec
1/2 ounce half & half

Free Pour

Splash vodka
Splash crème de cacao
Splash amaretto
Splash triple sec
Splash half & half

PALI BLUE BREEZE

Jigger

Fill blender with ice
2 ounces Malibu rum
1 ounce vodka
1 ounce Rose's Blue Raspberry Mix
2 ounces piña colada mix
1/2 ounce coconut milk

Free Pour

Fill blender with ice
2 counts Malibu rum
1 count vodka
1 count Rose's Blue Raspberry Mix
2 counts piña colada mix
Splash coconut milk

Blend until smooth. Mix 2 tablespoons of salt with 2 tablespoons of sugar
Coat rim of glass with salt and sugar mix. Garnish with a pineapple

Piña Colada

Planter's Punch

Purple Hooter
(Shot)

Rusty Nail

PIÑA COLADA

Jigger

Add 2 cups of ice to blender
3 ounces rum
2 ounces crème of coconut
2 ounces pineapple juice
Blend until smooth
Garnish with a pineapple slice

Free Pour

Add 2 cups of ice to the blender
3 counts rum
2 counts crème of coconut
2 counts of pineapple juice
Blend until smooth
Garnish with a pineapple slice

PLANTER'S PUNCH

Jigger

Fill glass with ice
2 ounces light rum
1 ounce dark rum
1 ounce orange juice
1 ounce cranberry juice
Stir to mix
Garnish with cherry

Free Pour

Fill glass with ice
2 counts light rum
1 count dark rum
1 count orange juice
1 count cranberry juice
Stir to mix
Garnish with cherry

PURPLE HOOTER (SHOT)

Jigger

1/2 ounce vodka
1/2 ounce Chambord
1/2 ounce cranberry juice

Free Pour

Splash vodka
Splash Chambord
Splash cranberry juice

RUSTY NAIL

Jigger

Fill glass with ice
1 1/2 ounces scotch
1/2 ounce Drambuie
Stir and serve

Free Pour

Fill glass with ice
1 count scotch
Splash of Drambuie
Stir and serve

Salty Dog

Sambuca

Sangria (Red)
Serves 24

Sangria (White)
Serves 24

SALTY DOG

Jigger

Salt the rim of the glass
Fill glass with ice
2 ounces vodka
2 ounces pineapple juice
Stir and serve

Free Pour

Salt the rim of the glass
Fill glass with ice
2 counts vodka
2 counts pineapple juice
Stir and serve

SAMBUCA

Jigger

2 ounces Sambuca
Drop 3 coffee beans into liqueur

Free Pour

2 counts Sambuca
Drop 3 coffee beans into liqueur

If desired, light liqueur on fire to "roast" coffee beans

SANGRIA (RED) SERVES 24

1/2 bottle of triple sec
1 bottle of brandy
6 bottles of red wine
2 cups of sugar
6 thinly sliced apples
6 thinly sliced pears
6 thinly sliced oranges
5 thinly sliced lemons
5 thinly sliced limes

Combine ingredients and marinate, preferably chilled, for 12 - 24 hours before serving.

Pour sangria into wine glasses or ladle into glasses, fruit included

SANGRIA (WHITE) SERVES 24

1/2 bottle of triple sec
1 bottle of brandy
6 bottles of white wine
2 cups of sugar
5 thinly sliced apples
5 thinly sliced pears
5 thinly sliced peaches
5 thinly sliced honeydew melon
5 thinly sliced lemons
5 thinly sliced limes

Combine ingredients and marinate, preferably chilled, for 12 - 24 hours before serving.

Pour sangria into wine glasses or ladle into glasses, fruit included

Screwdriver

Sea Breeze

Seven & Seven
(7&7)

Sex on the Beach

SCREWDRIVER

Jigger

Fill glass with ice
2 ounces vodka
2 ounces orange juice
Stir to mix then serve

Free Pour

Fill glass with ice
2 counts vodka
2 counts orange juice
Stir to mix then serve

SEA BREEZE

Jigger

Fill glass with ice
2 ounces vodka
1 ounce orange juice
1 ounce pineapple juice
Stir to mix then serve

Free Pour

Fill glass with ice
2 counts vodka
1 count orange juice
1 count pineapple juice
Stir to mix then serve

SEVEN & SEVEN (7&7)

Jigger

Fill glass with ice
2 ounces Seagrams 7
2 ounces 7 Up (or Sprite)
Stir to mix then serve

Free Pour

Fill glass with ice
2 counts Seagrams 7
2 counts 7 Up (or Sprite)
Stir to mix then serve

SEX ON THE BEACH

Jigger

Fill glass with ice
2 ounces vodka
1/2 ounce peach schnapps
1/2 ounce melon liqueur
1 ounce cranberry juice
1 ounce orange juice
Stir to mix and serve
Garnish with a cherry

Free Pour

Fill glass with ice
2 counts vodka
Splash peach schnapps
Splash melon liqueur
Splash cranberry juice
Splash orange juice
Stir to mix and serve
Garnish with a cherry

Shirley Temple
(Virgin)

Sidecar

Skirt

Sour
(anything)

SHIRLEY TEMPLE (VIRGIN)

Jigger

Fill glass with ice
6 ounces Sprite or 7Up
1 ounce grenadine
Several cherries to garnish

Free Pour

Fill glass with ice
Fill glass with Sprite or 7Up
Splash grenadine
Several cherries to garnish

SIDECAR

Jigger

Fill glass with ice
2 ounces brandy
1 ounce triple sec
1 tablespoon fresh lemon juice
Stir to mix
Garnish with a lemon twist

Free Pour

Fill glass with ice
2 counts brandy
1 count triple sec
Squeeze of two lemon wedges
Stir to mix
Garnish with a lemon twist

SKIRT

Jigger

Fill glass with ice
2 ounces brandy
1 ounce triple sec
1 ounce sweet n' sour
1 teaspoon sugar
1 teaspoon fresh lemon juice
Stir to mix
Garnish with lemon twist and cherry

Free Pour

Fill glass with ice
2 counts brandy
1 count triple sec
1 count sweet n' sour
Small spoonful of sugar
1 squeeze of lemon wedge
Stir to mix
Garnish with lemon twist and cherry

SOUR (ANYTHING)

Jigger

Fill glass with ice
2 ounces alcohol
2 ounces sweet n' sour
Garnish with cherry

Free Pour

Fill glass with ice
2 counts alcohol
2 counts sweet n' sour
Garnish with cherry

Spritzer

Strawberry Daiquiri
(Blended)

Strawberry Margarita
(Blended)

Stinger

SPRITZER

Jigger

4 ounces of chilled wine
(red or white)
2 ounces club soda

Free Pour

3/4 glass of chilled wine
(red or white)
Fill the rest of the glass with club soda

STRAWBERRY DAIQUIRI (BLENDED)

Jigger

Add 2 cups of ice to blender
3 ounces light rum
1 cup strawberries with sugar
1 ounce half & half
1/2 ounce sweet n' sour
Blend until smooth
Garnish with a strawberry

Free Pour

Add 2 cups of ice to blender the blender
3 counts light rum
1 cup strawberries with sugar
Splash half & half
1 count sweet n' sour
Blend until smooth
Garnish with a strawberry

STRAWBERRY MARGARITA (BLENDED)

Jigger

Add 2 cups of ice to blender
2 ounces tequila
1 cup strawberries with sugar
1/2 ounce of triple sec
1 ounces sweet n' sour
Squeeze of two lime wedges
Squeeze of two lemon wedges
Blend until smooth
Garnish with a lime

Free Pour

Add 2 cups of ice to the blender
3 counts tequila
1 cup strawberries with sugar
Splash of triple sec
1 counts sweet n' sour
Squeeze of two lime wedges
Squeeze of two lemon wedges
Blend until smooth
Garnish with a lime

STINGER

Jigger

Fill glass with ice
2 ounces brandy
1/2 ounce white crème de menthe
Stir to mix and serve

Free Pour

Fill glass with ice
2 counts brandy
Splash white crème de menthe
Stir to mix and serve

Tequila Maria

Tequila Sunrise

Toasted Almond

Tom Collins

TEQUILA MARIA

Jigger

Fill glass with ice
2 ounces tequila
Fill the rest of the glass with
Bloody Mary Mix
Shake once
Garnish with 2 olives and a lime

Free Pour

Fill glass with ice
2 counts tequila
Fill the rest of the glass with
Bloody Mary Mix
Shake once
Garnish with 2 olives and a lime

TEQUILA SUNRISE

Jigger

Fill glass with ice
1 measure tequila
Fill glass with orange juice
Drizzle grenadine into drink
Garnish with cherry

Free Pour

Fill glass with ice
2 counts tequila
Fill glass with orange juice
Drizzle grenadine into drink
Garnish with cherry

TOASTED ALMOND

Jigger

Fill glass with ice
1 ounce coffee liqueur
1 ounce amaretto
1 ounce half & half
Stir to mix then serve

Free Pour

Fill glass with ice
1 count coffee liqueur
1 count amaretto
1 count half & half
Stir to mix then serve

TOM COLLINS

Jigger

Fill glass with ice
2 ounces gin
1/2 packet sugar
1 ounce soda water
1/2 ounce Sprite or 7Up
1/2 ounce sweet n' sour
Teaspoon lemon juice
Garnish with lemon wedge
Stir to mix then serve

Free Pour

Fill glass with ice
2 counts gin
1/2 packet sugar
Splash soda water
Splash Sprite or 7Up
Splash sweet n' sour
Squeeze of lemon wedge
Garnish with lemon wedge
Stir to mix then serve

Tomahawk

Vodka Bull

Watermelon Martini

White Russian

TOMAHAWK

Jigger

Fill glass with ice
2 ounces vodka
1/2 ounce triple sec
1/2 ounce crème de cacao
1/2 ounce half & half
1/2 ounce lime juice
Stir to mix then serve

Free Pour

Fill glass with ice
2 counts vodka
Splash triple sec
Splash crème de cacao
Splash half & half
Squeeze of two lime wedges
Stir to mix then serve

VODKA BULL

Jigger

Fill shaker with ice
3 ounces vodka
1 ounce Red Bull energy drink
Shake and strain into glass

Free Pour

Fill shaker with ice
3 counts of vodka
Splash Red Bull energy drink
Shake and strain into glass

WATERMELON MARTINI

Jigger

Fill shaker with ice
3 ounces vodka
1 ounce watermelon liqueur
Tablespoon sweet n' sour
Shake and strain into glass

Free Pour

Fill shaker with ice
3 counts vodka
1 count watermelon liqueur
Splash sweet n' sour
Shake and strain into glass

WHITE RUSSIAN

Jigger

Fill glass with ice
Layer the ingredients
2 ounces vodka
1 ounce Kahlua
1 ounce half & half

Free Pour

Fill glass with ice
Layer the ingredients
2 counts vodka
1 count Kahlua
Splash half & half

Virgin Strawberry Daiquiri

Virgin Strawberry Margarita

Virgin Long Island Iced tea

Virgin Mai Tai

VIRGIN STRAWBERRY DAIQUIRI

Jigger

Add 2 cups of ice to blender
1 cup strawberries with sugar
1/2 ounce half & half
1/2 ounce coconut milk
1 ounce sweet n' sour
Blend until smooth
Garnish with a strawberry

Free Pour

Add 2 cups of ice to the blender
1 cup strawberries with sugar
Splash half & half
1/2 ounce coconut milk
1 count sweet n' sour
Blend until smooth
Garnish with a strawberry

VIRGIN STRAWBERRY MARGARITA

Jigger

Add 2 cups of ice to blender
1 cup strawberries with sugar
1 ounce sweet n' sour
Squeeze of two lime wedges
Squeeze of two lemon wedges
Blend until smooth
Garnish with a lime

Free Pour

Add 2 cups of ice to the blender
1 cup strawberries with sugar
1 counts sweet n' sour
Squeeze of two lime wedges
Squeeze of two lemon wedges
Blend until smooth
Garnish with a lime

VIRGIN LONG ISLAND ICED TEA

Jigger

Fill glass with ice
2 ounces lemonade
2 ounces sweet n' sour
2 ounces Coke
Stir to mix and serve

Free Pour

Fill glass with ice
2 counts lemonade
2 counts sweet n' sour
2 counts Coke
Stir to mix and serve

VIRGIN MAI TAI

Jigger

Fill glass with ice
1/2 ounce pineapple juice
1/2 ounce orange juice
1/2 ounce sweet n' sour
1/2 ounce grenadine
Stir to mix
Garnish with a lime and cherry

Free Pour

Fill glass with ice
Splash pineapple juice
Splash orange juice
Splash sweet n' sour
Splash grenadine
Stir to mix
Garnish with a lime and cherry